P9-CCQ-856

# *I'LL TRADE YOU AN ELK*

*by*
*Charles A. Goodrum*

*Funk & Wagnalls*
A DIVISION OF READER'S DIGEST BOOKS, INC.
*New York*

TO THE NEXT GENERATION:

*Chris, Julie, and Geoffrey*

2

A portion of this book appeared originally in *The New Yorker*, in different form. And another portion appeared originally in *The Atlantic Monthly*, also in different form.


Library of Congress Catalog Card Number: 67-16225
Printed in the United States of America

# Contents


1 *He Said It Was a Pelican* 1
2 *Noah and the PR Man* 17
3 *Mostly Alligators* 34
4 *Discord* 50
5 *Resolution* 56
6 *Tiglath-Pileser* 76
7 *Incident at the Lion House* 96
8 *The Joad Family Returns* 119
9 *The Dog Census* 140
10 *The Incubator* 154
11 *Of All Small Things* 175
12 *Fearful Symmetry* 198
13 *Epilogue* 217

# 1

## *He Said It Was a Pelican*

In the late Nineteen Thirties my father found himself in charge of a zoo. It was a small zoo—pitiful, springs to mind—but it had all the parts: a lion house, a bird house, an alligator pit, eight bear dens, and a duck pond. It was surrounded with two hundred acres of parkland and in my father's eyes its future lay all before it.

My father knew no more about running a zoo than the next ex-schoolteacher. Through fairly logical steps, he had started as a YMCA secretary in southeastern Kansas, had gone on to Kansas City as Assistant Scout Executive, became a coach, and at this point, when I was fifteen, had become The Director of Recreation for the City of Wichita, Kansas.

Father had been hired by a huge, red-haired and red-faced Scotch forester named Alfred MacDonald who was the Director of Parks for Wichita. MacDonald had come to the prairie soon after the First World War with an incredible dedication to make a place of beauty out of this windswept town. In the space of twenty years he had in fact created as lovely a series of parks and woodlands as there existed between St. Louis and Denver. What should have been a delight and satisfaction with his accomplishment, however, was flawed by a deep and burning distress: he resented people in general and people in his parks in particular. His position in the feud was that he had had enough trouble getting stuff to grow, Heaven knew, without having the place overrun with the high-heeled and tennis-shod masses.

This fury so preyed upon him that a leisurely Sunday drive through the park system would bring him to the quivering edge of apoplexy and by the fall of 1936 his devoted secretary began to fear for his health. She had long since tried reason and seen it fail. She had tried to keep him bodily out of the parks (especially on weekends), but the parks were his whole life and this got her nowhere. But in the early spring of 1937, as she dutifully read the park professional journals, she found a new fad had broken out in the trade. Suddenly there was a burst of articles about a new form of public servant called a "recreation director." This innovation proved to be a variety of activist who was paid to *organize* public play. He established tournaments and handicrafts and outdoor joys and saw to it that "parks were really used—not just looked at!" A few of the eastern cities had experimented with the idea, but to read the literature, you'd think the technique had swept the country.

In any event, the lady fell on it with a rush, convinced that here at last was the solution she sought. It took her only five months of hard labor to convince MacDonald that he too should try the experiment, one time. The fact was he was sure it wouldn't work, and even if it would Wichita wasn't ready for it, but the only way he saw to get this charming—and indispensable—lady off his back was to let the thing fail and be done with it. He capitulated. He gritted his teeth and let the word out. My father heard the call in the Chanute City Schools, abandoned schoolteaching, and we were in Wichita.

Within hours of his arrival, Father knew where he stood. While MacDonald still questioned the need for his new assistant, he was too careful with the taxpayers' money to let the job go to waste, so he clarified matters at once. Between the Director of Parks and the Director of Recreation there was to be a simple division of labor: if it grew it belonged to MacDonald. If it worked, it was Father's. In this way the boss got the parkways, the lakes, and the parks themselves. Father got the tennis courts, the swimming pools, all the picnic grounds, outdoor theaters, baseball diamonds—and the zoo. The zoo was far and away Father's favorite.

It was the summer of 1938 that we took our first innocent steps toward animal chaos. The summer of '38 was even hotter than usual for Kansas and that is not easy. Kansas has a heat that has to be felt to be believed, and having experienced it few people can bring themselves to talk much about it afterwards. The Kansas winter is dedicated to successive blizzards that spread a sheet of ice from Nebraska to the Oklahoma border; then, about the middle of March, the sun appears in a blinding flash. It proceeds to fry the snow away in a steady blast which goes straight into the desert heat of July, skipping spring completely. By midsummer the heat is shimmering off the pavement, and the sky has turned to a brilliant yellow-whiteness that pulses at your eyeballs. Through it all there is the twenty-mile-an-hour wind peeling the scalp from the head. Carveth Wells, the explorer, once said the only place he knew as bitterly hot as Wichita was Cairo, Egypt, and in Cairo they dressed for it.

On one of these July afternoons I was home in our basement, stripped to my shorts with two fans blowing on me, when the phone rang upstairs. I struggled up and it was my father.

"How'd you like to take a run out in the country?"

The thought of the heat boiling off the wheat stubble paralyzed me.

"Well, I'm pretty busy. Do you need some help or something?"

"Not especially. We just got a call from a farmer near Haven who says he's caught a pelican and he wonders if we want it for the zoo."

"A pelican? Is that possible?"

"Hardly. He's probably got some kind of a crane or heron, but I thought it might be worth looking into. Might be something we could use in the Bird House. Want to come along?"

Father was clearly excited and he wanted to share what looked like fun to him and I didn't have the heart to refuse.

"OK. Do you want me to come downtown?"

"No. I'll be right out."

I had barely gotten dressed and onto the porch swing when he arrived in the family Plymouth instead of one of the park trucks, as I'd expected. I got in and we headed northwest out of town. The heat was even worse than I'd feared. The tires hissed as they stuck to the soft asphalt, and the wind whipped the glare off the wheat fields straight into your face. If you touched the window sills of the car, they seared the skin and what wasn't burned was pricked by the pile on the upholstery. The sun was blinding. Father's enthusiasm steadily ebbed away and his conversation got shorter and shorter. By the time we passed Belle Plaine I was miserable and Father was so irritated I was afraid the bird might turn out to be a thin goose and he'd hang one on the poor farmer. Just as we neared the breaking point, the proper homestead appeared and we pulled in off the highway.

It was a typical Kansas layout. It had the white house in front with the silver-painted tin roof. There were two unpainted sheds and a faded red barn in back. The one tree stood out in the cattle yard with a half-dozen limp cows packed into its shade. We stopped the car in the dust driveway and as we got out the farmer came off his porch to join us.

"You the zoo man?" he asked.

"I'm from the Park Department," Father replied in an unusually flat tone for him. "I understand you've got some kind of a bird."

"It's a pelican! Found 'im out front on the road. Just lyin' there. I told the wife, there's a dead pelican out'n the road. We went out and looked at it and it was the biggest damn thing I ever saw. I didn't want to leave it there to get run over so I drug it back of the house and on the way it begun to flap aroun'n raise hell. I got 'im into the feed room and turned 'im loose and he's in there now. You got a cage or something?"

"We can handle it if we want it," Father replied. "May we look at it, please? We'll need to know precisely what kind of a specimen it is to see if we can use it." Father was already laying the ground for a rejection.

"It's a pelican I tol' ya! Come on, I'll show him to ya."

We followed the man through the dust to the barn where he opened a door and we stepped in past him. The barn was astonishingly cool and it took us a moment to focus in the gloom. When we finally could see again, we found the farmer had crossed the building and was peering through some cracks in the wooden walls of a small room. We joined him and squinted too and found ourselves looking into the red eye of the biggest, maddest pelican I had ever seen. He stood nearly shoulder high and was striding around on three-foot mounds of loose wheat, the very epitome of outraged dignity. He seemed to know he was being watched and he would snap his head from side to side trying to see who was behind the boards.

"Why he's tremendous!" Father was delighted. "He'll be a wonderful addition! You'll be able to *give* him to us? I'm afraid we haven't any money to buy anything with."

"Hell, yes! Take 'im! What use've I got for a pelican? I

wouldn't even know what to feed him." (Father didn't know either, but he hoped he could find out before the bird expired. This idea reminded him that in this heat time mattered and it galvanized him into action.)

"Chuck, go out to the trunk and bring in the gunny sacks there. Has he been given any water?"

"How could I give 'im water?"

"Well, could we put a bucket in the grain bin?"

"Not without ruinin' a lot of wheat."

"You'd rather not?"

"We ain't putting water in the feed bin."

"Right." Father abandoned the idea as I reached the door and headed out into the glare.

I ran to the car, and got the keys out of the ignition and unlocked the trunk. Inside I found a thick bundle of clean feed sacks, lying as smooth as if they'd been ironed, but still smelling of bran. I grabbed up the mound and sprinted back toward the barn with the sweat pouring down my face and making my shirt stick to me like tape. Inside again, I delivered the stuff to Father and waited for the word on how we were to proceed.

"I think the best bet is for you and me to get in there with the bird, and this gentleman can close the door behind us—and let us out fast if we need to! By the way, I'm Bernie Goodrum." Father offered a hand to the farmer.

"Howard Walker."

"Glad to meet you. This is my boy, Charles." Much handshaking and then Father picked up two of the sacks and gave me one.

"Now let's go in after him. I'll get his attention and you jump him from behind. You pin his wings down and then I'll slip a bag over his head."

I squinted back between the cracks and noted with great clarity that the bill was at least a foot and a half long and came to a sharp hook on the end. Every so often the bird would slip on the wheat and would open his wings out to catch himself. This revealed a wingspread of better than ten feet and they looked as though they could do substantial damage. Making a quick choice between being pecked to death and beaten to a pulp, I chose the latter and let Father's plan stand. It wasn't so much that I had so little interest in collecting the bird as it was that I was scared to death of it. There seemed no honorable escape, however, so I squeezed into the bin after Father. The farmer slammed the door behind us.

The pelican backed up a bit on the hill of wheat, keeping us in front of him and making sharp swipes with his beak while throwing his wings out to steady himself. Father began to make passes at his head, using the sack like a cape, while I circled around the walls of the little room. The whole thing took on the rhythm of running under water since you'd sink into the wheat up to your shins with every step and have to heave yourself out to go forward. Fortunately, the pelican weighed over fifty pounds and he was having as much trouble as we were.

We proceeded to struggle slowly around in a sort of ritual dance until I was off his left flank. Father began to jerk his sack around frantically and flip it toward the bird's eyes, and the latter finally gave up trying to keep track of us both and began to concentrate on ripping up the cloth in earnest. I staggered slowly up to the bird and when I got to what looked like a body's length from him I said, "I'm going to jump and try to land on his back. I'll try to get my arms around him, but you'll grab his beak before he gets me, hunh?"

"Right. You count and jump on three and I'll grab at the same time."

We both edged a bit closer, I yelled the numbers and leapt. "Oofed" would be more accurate if there were such a word. Everything we did was in such slow motion that the bird knew quite well what was coming, but he was having so much trouble slithering through the grain that he couldn't get braced for any defense. We all landed in a heap together, and what with my covering my face against the bird, I never really knew who did what to whom, but when I dared look there was a sack completely over the bird's head and Father seemed to be hanging on to the beak like a handle. I had the wings pinned against his body and the farmer staggered in to join us and got another bag around the breast. We then struggled back into the open part of the barn in a tight cluster and the farmer let go long enough to get some twine. He tied the bird's feet and we slid the bird into a sack from the bottom, tying it around his neck, outside Father's original hood.

Still walking as a trio, we carried the bird out to the car and laid him on the floor of the rear seat. We were sure he'd never survive a trip in the airless trunk. At this point Father pulled the sack off the head and there he leaned, bagged from the neck down and madder than ever. He appeared to consider the situation very deliberately and once he had concluded there was no escape he refused to struggle. He slammed his "chin" down on the back seat, gave us a furious glance, and lay there snapping his beak together like someone drumming on a table in fury.

We stepped back and congratulated ourselves.

"Want some lemonade?" the farmer asked in a burst of camaraderie.

"Thank you, no," Father replied, all graciousness. "I think we'd best get the bird into a pond as quickly as possible. I would like to see where you found him, though."

"Come on out to the road."

We followed Walker onto the highway and he pointed off to the West.

"Right there'n the middle, spread out'n a heap."

It was suddenly clear what had happened. The black asphalt stretched away like a watery ribbon of silver, so bright it was uncomfortable to look at. The heat waves shimmered back and forth and you could picture that poor bird flying over parched stubble and suddenly spotting this stretch of "water" — long and thin, but clearly wet — the first moisture he'd seen in who knew how long. He'd come in for a cooling swim with his feet forward, bounced once and knocked himself cold.

"What was a pelican doin' here in the first place?" Walker asked.

"I can't imagine. They have wild pelicans in the Mississippi bottoms, I know, and I think they're sometimes seen along the Rocky Mountain flyway. This one seems awfully far inland, though. He must have gotten sidetracked onto some tributary and kept making wrong turns till he ended up here on the high plains. Fantastic! We'd better roll, now. That bird deserves better treatment. He's got to have water. Many thanks to you and come and see him in the waterfowl pond!"

We exchanged the usuals and headed back to town at top speed. I rode backward to keep a sympathetic eye on the passenger, but his distaste for me never wavered. We headed straight for the zoo where we were met by the two keepers, and among us we got the bird unloaded and then unsacked by the pond. With everybody hanging on to an extremity to keep him immobilized, Father clipped off the pinion feathers on one wing and we heaved him loose over the fence. (He was wing-clipped, of course, to keep him from flying away. Losing the first "finger feathers" makes the lift of the two wings so uneven that when the bird strokes to fly, it throws it off balance and keeps it from getting airborne.)

He never lost his dignity. He struggled to his feet, shook out his feathers, and looked around. The pond was a lovely, cool spot surrounded by grass and great overhanging elms, and the pelican promptly detected the water. He swept toward it and plunged in with the look of something attempted, something done. Father headed for the public library to see what pelicans ate and I took a bus home.

By the time we gathered at the supper table in the evening, I assumed that the pelican episode was closed and we would resume the even tenor of our family in summer. Not so. Father had scarcely stormed into the kitchen than we got the new picture. Rather than the bird representing a cheap find for the bird pond, Father saw it as the foundation stone for one of the great zoological collections of North America.

"Mae, did you hear about the pelican?"

"Yes, wasn't that lucky! Charles told me how you caught it. But you should have taken one of the men with you, Bernie. And don't they have a net or something for that sort of thing?"

"No, no! That's not the point at all. What I mean is, that bird is going to be the thin edge of the wedge for us. You just watch, now. There was real human interest stuff there and it'll get us some good newspaper coverage. Then as soon as we get a little publicity, people will start coming to see that bird and visiting the zoo. As soon as we get people interested, we can generate community support, and we can start building up the collection. We can go to the Rotarians and the Kiwanians and the Masons and get each one of 'em to give a display. We'll make 'em each a big bronze sign in front, like: 'This Monkey Island Given to the Children of Wichita by the Wichita Lions Club.' "

"*They* ought'a give you a herd of lions. How about a pack of camels from the Shriners?" Father's look showed I wasn't funny.

"Once this thing gets started, there's no end to it. There's no reason why Wichita shouldn't be known all over the Middle West for its zoo. When you think of the great zoos of the country, what do you think of?"

"St. Louis? New York and Chicago?" I suggested, missing the point again.

"No! There're those, but there's Swope Park in Kansas City, and there's the San Diego Zoo — one of the finest in the nation. There's Catalina's Bird Farm and the Broadmoor Hotel's collection, and how about what they're doing all over Florida? You don't have to be a big city to support one of these things. What you need is a little imagination and a lot of civic spirit and before you know it you've got something that's the pride of a whole region. And there's no reason why Wichita can't have the showplace of the mid-continent area!"

There was a great silence around the table. We had heard the general theme of this before, but until now there was a sort of wouldn't-it-be-wonderful air about it and it made pleasant conversation. Tonight there was a clear-cut shift from the theoretical to the applied. No one said anything for just a bit too long and then Mother decided she'd better introduce a shred of reality into the talk.

"Do you think Mr. MacDonald would like your doing all this so soon?"

"There's nothing succeeds like success! If I can get this started it'll take off by itself. By the time he realizes where it's headed, it'll be moving too fast to stop it."

"But do you think he really wants to have a big zoo here, dear? That isn't the sort of thing he likes, is it?"

"Look, the park's there. Now we've got that little zoo in the midst of all that grass and trees. There's plenty of room for expansion right where it is. He wouldn't have to start anything new—just go on with what he's got. The point is, he admits himself the parks should be *used*. A good zoo is the perfect focus for a park system. It appeals to everybody in town. The adults bring the kids, folks without kids can picnic by the river and visit after they've eaten. The high school crowd'll have some place to go instead of just driving around. And it'll be a tourist attraction and bring people in from the trade area. You can get a better return on your dollar in a thing like this than anything else you can invest in."

Father suddenly stopped talking, glanced quickly at Mother to see if she'd caught the slip, and then began to eat very earnestly. Mother was kind enough to leave it alone, but Father had produced the pin which would explode his balloon before it rose from the ground. Money.

Even if he could get someone else to build him a zoo, once it was there the animals had to be fed and the cages cleaned. This meant food which had to be bought and keepers who had to be paid. And it was manifest in our household that here was the harsh note of reality.

Wichita in '38 was seven years into The Depression and while a couple of years before it looked like we might be coming out of it, the wreckage from the Droughts and the Dust Bowl was still hanging on and Wichita was nearly as bad off as at the beginning of the catastrophe. Families of fellow employees still talked about the years when the city revenues weren't enough to meet the monthly payrolls. Dozens of people had been furloughed or fired outright until even the protective services had been cut too deeply for a while. With the memory still sharp of days when the fire stations were undermanned and the police department was on twelve-hour shifts to cover lost positions, the chance of getting funds to feed a bunch of monkeys was powerfully slight.

The truth of this was hard for Father to grasp because his own natural optimism made it quite unreal to him. Even in the days when the school system was paying him in scrip because tax receipts were insufficient to cover the checks, Father was blithely unconcerned. It'll all sort itself out, he was convinced. By the end of the Thirties, he was confident that the worst was definitely behind us and that from here on, every thing was getting better, faster, every day.

While it did begin to look like he might be right, the community was still so shaken by the past seven years that they no longer trusted what would happen next. Without faith in the next month, much less the next year, Father's perpetual flights of assurance got nowhere with his friends or bosses — or his family. Today, to Father, was always as bad as it was going to get. To Mother and me, today—any day—was an astonishingly good piece of luck which was unlikely to be repeated. Money ruined all of my Father's conversations because no one found it as trivial as he did.

We ate in silence and I was depressed as usual with the feeling that no one ever supported Father on anything. Frantically trying to think of something to say, I remembered the pelican and asked loudly, "Did you find out what to feed the bird?"

Father brightened at once. "I did! I discovered the best thing for them is fish, of course. But if you don't have that available," (I noticed he'd avoided, "if you can't afford that") "they'll do just about as well on turkey mash. We mixed up a batch and shoved it in and I thought the Canadian geese were going to get it all before the pelican even noticed it, but he finally saw what they were doing. He must have put away five pounds before he was through. He's going to be fine. I've called the papers. They'll be out tomorrow."

# 2

# *Noah and the PR Man*

There is next to nothing simpler than getting a zoo story into a local newspaper. Even surer than sex is the little furry animal bit. "Nice Ice For The Polar Pair." "Zoo News From The New Gnus." There is something about the theme that brings out the best in the caption writer—and there seems to be no paper so dignified it can resist it. I still recall the shock I had after the war when I was doing graduate work at Columbia. I opened the *New York Times* to find a story about the Bronx zoo constructing a shelter for their platypus next door to the panda's cage. The headline read: "New Platypusery To Rise By Pandamonium." It subverts the strongest.

Wichita's two papers were no different. A zoo story was a noncontroversial, good (cheap) source of human interest stuff. All it took was something new—baby, beast, house, or whatever—and they were glad to oblige. The pitiful thing about it was that our zoo hadn't had a new anything (with the exception of an endless stream of black bears) for so long that the papers had given up looking for stories. Thus the press never came around, and without the usual news reminders, most of the citizens had forgotten the town even had a zoo.

The pelican, trivial as it was, reversed the process with an impact out of all proportion to its worth. Both the Wichita *Beacon* (evening) and the Wichita *Eagle* (morning and evening) showed up with reporters and photographers. Shots were taken and interviews held. On the following day the resulting stories, pictures, and snappy headlines turned up in prime space. And suddenly 100,000 of the city's 120,000 citizens learned there was a zoo in one of the parks, and to a man were struck with a great truth. Primitive syllogism as seen by local citizen: There was a man who had a pelican that he did not want so he gave it to the zoo. The zoo took this pelican the man did not want. Therefore the zoo will take all things that men do not want. At last, a way to get rid of that goddam parakeet! Within four hours Father had thirty-five parakeets, two cockatiels, twenty-one canaries, and two black crows. Father called home to say he was too busy to make lunch. He was exuberant.

During the afternoon he inherited nearly two dozen rabbits, many pregnant, and sixteen guinea pigs, most of them paired. He got ex-ducklings left over from the past Easter, the Easter before that, and Easters two, three, and four years back. Children, parents, and grandparents appeared with pet squirrels in boxes, cages, cartons, and paper sacks. By the time Father got home for a very late supper, he was beside himself.

"Mae, it is fantastic! You wouldn't believe the stuff that's coming in. You could hardly find a parking place over there all day long. The mob got so thick by 11:00 that we finally set up a receiving station in the Lion House. We put a picnic table out in the middle of the room and lined the people up in front of it and the line was through the doors half the time. It's simply amazing. Charles, I want you to come over tomorrow and help out for a while. We assume most of the stuff has come in, but we thought we'd leave the setup as it is, just in case. I've had Bob Saylor taking the stuff in, but I need him now to fix up space for what we got."

We sat down at the supper table again and Mother asked, "What are you doing with it all? Do you have places for everything?"

"We've put 'em everywhere. Jim set up boards on the floor in the feeding kitchen and we've got a square full of guinea pigs and white mice in one corner and a mess of turtles in another. The rabbits are running loose in the tool shed, and we've just been throwing the ducks and geese over the fence into the waterfowl pond. We closed the Bird House down and turned loose a fine peacock to run around in the aisles for the time being. The birds are the worst. The Bird House is so crummy I'm afraid it has mites and the little birds can't tolerate that. So we're having to leave them in the Lion House in whatever they came in till we can work something out. I pulled off the second shift lifeguards at Woodland and College Hill and they've been rounding up packing crates all over town. We thought we'd put hardware cloth over 'em tomorrow and at least merge the mess some. We got some beautiful stuff, though. Those cockatiels are easily worth a hundred dollars a pair."

"What did you do with them?"

"Well, they ought to go in the Bird House, but I'm afraid to take a chance till we can do something about the building. They're still in their cage on top of the refrigerator."

Father had two outdoor programs due to start at eight o'clock so he dashed off leaving me with instructions to be at the zoo a little before it opened at nine the next morning. By the time I went to bed the temperature had dropped to nearly ninety and I went to sleep recalling the Lion House was usually cooler than it had a right to be.

Next morning I got rolling at a fairly decent hour and took an early bus downtown and then transferred to a northbound local which dropped me off at the edge of Riverside Park. This was one of the first installations MacDonald had developed, and it was a wide, shaded area spread out in a fan of land made by a bend in the Little Arkansas River. Its oaks and elms and cottonwoods were full-grown by now, and at this time in the morning the sun was throwing huge shadows across the heavily watered lawns. Being deeply impressed by Howard Pyle illustrations at the time, I thought this must be the way Sherwood Forest looked just before breakfast.

The zoo buildings were scattered among the trees about a block away, and I took off along the usual curving sidewalks which have been indigenous to every park since Eden. I passed through the entrance gates and had barely refocused to navigate a curbing when a large white goat shot out of the shadows and lunged straight at me. I leaped off into the street with some idea of grabbing his horns as he came by when he was suddenly yanked up short by a rope. I scanned the latter carefully and it seemed to be firmly tied to the base of a light-fixture on the back of the stone gate.

We stood and glared at each other for a moment while I tried to sort out the picture. There was the possibility that the goat belonged to the zoo and was used to keep the grass down in some inaccessible place, but if so, the city was begging for a law suit. This tied threat kept jerking around, trying to get at me, and the hair was up on his neck with the look of a goat mad from arguments long past. The other possibility was that this was a donation like Father's rabbits and guinea pigs and if so, the size was going up dramatically. I knew the reason I was supposed to be there was to "acquisition" these gifts, but I quickly decided to make note of this item and report it to someone a good deal bigger than I was. The rope was too short for him to get much grass and there was no water in range, so somebody was going to have to work on this one fairly soon.

I circled the beast, which kept straining at me the while, and walked on down the street. Working my way past the bear pits and Bird House, I could see a crowd up ahead, gradually collecting outside the entrance to the Lion House. The closer I got the clearer it was that this was more of yesterday. Everybody was either carrying a cardboard box or had some kind of bird cage hanging from a hand. One very tall man had a tiny monkey sitting on his shoulder and the monkey was chewing on the man's necktie in a bored sort of way. I took a short cut around to the back and tried the door to the feeding kitchen in the rear.

The Lion House was far and away the finest building in the park, and served as a sort of focus and centerpiece for the present (and Father's projected) zoo plan. It had been built in the early Twenties from some plans left over after the Columbian Exposition of '92 so it ran rather heavily to neoclassic, but it was astonishingly functional and quite attractive. It had a green tiled roof over its center hall (smacking slightly of an opaque botanical garden), and then twelve large cages, each half inside and half outdoors, distributed down the sides of the building. The exterior was of soft glazed brick with the interior emphasizing antiseptic white tile with green designs. It was light, spacious, and amazingly well ventilated.

The feeding kitchen, for which I was headed, was hidden from the public at the rear of the display hall, and I remembered it as a light, airy room, tiled like an operating theater and filled with a peaceful quiet. One side was taken up with a walk-in refrigerator which held the weekly horse carcass, the center held the chopping block and a metal-covered table for mixing food, and the far side had a gas range where the appropriate foods were cooked to mash. The few times I had seen it before, there had been three or four fire department chairs by the table, and being the warmest place in winter and the coolest in summer it served as headquarters for the zoo's two keepers.

On this morning, I eased the back door open cautiously and found no one in sight but the air filled with a haze of high-pitched squeaks and cheeps and scratchings. As I slipped into the room, I could see the boards and pens Father had described and there were the hordes of little animals he'd reported. You could barely make out the floor or the walls for the coating of fur and feathers churning around. The feeling of being about to step on something no matter where you stood gave a slight sense of vertigo, so I worked my way across to the main lion room and carefully shut the connecting doors behind me.

The big room was much quieter, and, except for a certain amount of activity in one of the monkey cages on the left, everything was peaceful. Of the ten cages, only eight were occupied. On the right, Simba, the big male lion, and his young son, owned the first two cages. The middle cage was left empty for transferring in and out of during cleaning, the fourth cage held a pair of black leopards, and two cheetahs had the one nearest to the kitchen.

The cages on the left side were intended for somewhat smaller cats, but our poverty had converted these to cages for monkeys. In various combinations, they consisted of two fine spider monkeys, two smallish baboons, a half dozen common rhesus, and two capuchins. Except for the rhesus, they all looked sort of lost in their environment. But they did look healthy. With the single exception of a three-legged black bear, there was not a specimen in the zoo that was not in excellent and cheerful condition. They had that sleek, shiny, well-fed look that made them a pleasure to watch.

The big picnic table was still there in the center of the room, and I picked up the clip-board that lay on it. There, sheet on sheet, was the report of the previous day's take, all noted down in Bob Saylor's deliberate Irish hand. His entries were neatly catalogued: Description of animal, type, condition, and name. Donor's name and address. Special instructions. The special instructions were a mixture of the obvious (Chippy, a squirrel, likes nuts; Peter, a rabbit, eats carrots, lettuce, and cabbage), and the poignant. Among the latter were ways the animal liked to be petted, what frightened it, where it had been found and how it had been cared for. As I read these I was torn with a desire to search out that particular gift and wish it welcome—plus an irritation at the owners, that if they thought so much of their pet why had they "dumped" it at the zoo?

I heard the door open and looked around. Bob Saylor had come in. Father had inherited Bob as the Head Keeper, since he was the only one who knew anything about the zoo business—or to be more accurate—about taking care of the animals. Bob had no idea whatsoever about veterinary medicine or zoo management, but his predecessor had told *him* what each animal ate and he proceeded to duplicate it efficiently. Saylor was helped by a tall, silent Negro named Jim Poindexter who had worked on the zoo grounds as a WPA man and when Saylor's original helper had disappeared, Jim had asked for the job. They both had a strange detachment about the animals they cared for. They kept them spotlessly clean and well-fed and talked to them in a matter-of-fact voice, but neither one of them showed any particular affection for them. This surprised me when I first met it, since I expected a deep bond between keeper and charge, but I later realized that the main thing that was lacking was the little-furry-animal kind of talk. The men liked the work and enjoyed the animals, but they never confused routine characteristics with personality. This distressed Father no end, but he hadn't figured out what to do about it.

Saylor's immediate impression was one of great gravity and concentration. He was small, balding, and had a tense look about him which may have resulted from the fact that his skin was stretched so tightly across his forehead and cheek bones that it seemed to be polished at the corners. Bob had a curious mannerism. When he spoke to people or read, he would throw his head back as if he were seeing through very small bifocals. Inasmuch as he never wore glasses and had never even owned a pair, this always struck me as having a certain flair to it.

"Howdy, son," he said. "Your dad said you might come over. We can sure use you."

"Morning, Mr. Saylor. I've been reading your records. You must have fifty or sixty things down here."

"Lord, yes. I'm going crazy just throwing food into the pens and trying to find something that'll hold water. I've got jar lids and tin cans and breakfast bowls and I'm barely half through. The birds are the worst. We've got the animals in bunches, but most of the birds are by themselves and I can't keep up with them."

"Do you think the worst is past or are you going to get many more?"

"There's a pack of 'em outside right now. I think your dad's bit off more'n he can chew here, but maybe he knows what he's doin'."

"Let's hope so," I answered and then remembered, "Oh there's a goat tied to the Sims Street entrance. I guess they meant to give it to you. Somebody ought to bring it in or something." I didn't want to admit I was afraid of it, so I let it hang at this point. "Do I need to know anything about this acquisition business? Do we take everything they give us, regardless?"

"That's what your dad says. He says even if we don't want it it's good advertising for the zoo and they'll tell their friends and all that. He says we maybe can use some of the stuff and what we don't want we can give away."

"Do you think so too, Mr. Saylor?"

"Rather not say."

It was now nine o'clock and he unlocked the doors. From there on the day deteriorated into one great confusion. I got a line started and then put on my best public smile and asked, "How do you do, can I help you?" This pulled the plug and for eight solid hours I got the story. They had seen an article in the paper that said the zoo was anxious to get new animals. Well, about a year ago we bought this canary . . . baby alligator . . . deodorized skunk, and well, the children don't take as good care of it as they should . . . I'm on the road so much . . . et cetera. Similarly, my brother was out hunting and he found this baby raccoon, terrapin, possum, what-have-you, and he brought it home with him. . . . I'd try to appear grateful for the gift and I'd write down all the information with genuine care. I wasn't sure just which clue was needed, either. They'd shove a box or cage at me, I'd peek in, note down its condition from a lay point of view, and then deposit it against the rear wall. At irregular intervals Bob Saylor would appear, scoop up as many specimens as he could carry, and disappear.

It soon became apparent that while yesterday's haul could be pictured as coming out of dining rooms and off back porches, today's catch ran more to the significant and valuable. Mixed in with the usual squirrels, rabbits, and turtles, were occasional parrots and finches. There was a beautiful sulfur-crested cockatoo. We were obviously getting too many 'coons, possums, and skunks, but there were also a few that could be splendid specimens if we could ever find a place for them — we got a fine badger, a moth-eaten coyote, and, of course, the tiny monkey I'd seen waiting to come in. Each animal had his own story.

The monkey had come from Mexico and had been with this man for several years. The owner was a petroleum geologist and there was deep and genuine affection between the two, but the geologist found the small one more and more of a burden to take from job to job and when he read about the pelican he saw the zoo as a genuine haven for an old friend. Their parting was so agonizing that I finally had to leave them and go to find Saylor. I brought him in and we decided for the moment to give the central cleaning cage on the monkey side over to the little fellow. He was almost too small to be held by the bars, but not quite, and we slipped him in the door in the hope that the monkeys on either side and our continued presence might ease his loneliness until we got things sorted out. He looked as lost in that huge space as he actually was.

The most spectacular acquisition was a pair of magnificent macaws brought in by an elderly couple, each carrying a tall floor perch. These birds stood four feet long from crest to tail and were a brilliant red with purple and green head feathers and bright yellow bills. They clung to their perches with considerable nonchalance and occasionally would lift a blue foot to adjust some ruffled feather. The gentleman who presented them explained that they had originally sat in the lobby of Loew's Midland Theater in Kansas City and I immediately recalled the palms and fountains of its Spanish waiting room. They had stood there adding color through the Twenties, but when the Crash came the pipe organ inside and the macaws without were the first to go. This man was the chief usher and his wife had worked in one of the box offices until the Great Readjustment. When they had been laid off they were given the birds and had cared for them ever since. The elderly gentleman was now working for a sign painting company, but they were worried about what might happen to the birds if something happened to the couple themselves. As negligible as my zoological knowledge was at that time, even I could recall having read somewhere that parrots live eighty to a hundred years and I could understand their concern. I told them with real sincerity that these birds would be the finest displays in our Bird House and that they should come often to see them. I took their names as I had everyone else's, but I felt sure that Father would want to look them up and talk to them about the birds. They left with assurances that they'd be back.

The fact was that about two-thirds of the people were stricken with conscience as they'd hand over the family duck or parakeet and want to know where they could come to see it later. Knowing that Father's justification for absorbing this onslaught was to advertise the zoo and stimulate attendance, I blithely assured each one that just as soon as we got things sorted out their pet would be among its appropriate peers and for them to be sure to visit it. I knew that we were bearing toward 200 this-and-thats by late afternoon and I could not even picture where the stuff was going. Saylor and later two young lifeguard types would disappear through the door lugging out a couple of cages or cartons and soon come back for more.

Father had come in about noon with a sack lunch for me and offered to spell me at the table while I ate. He was still excited by the development and got into far more animated conversations with the donors than I managed. By the time I rejoined him, however, the enormity of what was happening was beginning to get through to him. The line was shortening but there was never a real break — and he could see that this thing was beginning to reach crisis proportions.

I had asked Father if Mr. MacDonald knew about it yet and he had admitted that he hadn't "had the opportunity to discuss it with him," but he was tearing up so much of the lifeguard and greenskeeper schedules borrowing people to help out for a few hours that this couldn't last too much longer. Father couldn't stay for long since he had an exhibition by a visiting pro going on at the golf course, but just before he left he was dealt a sobering piece of news.

"Bernie," Bob Saylor let him know, "little before noon one of those reporters was out here to see how the pelican was doin'. Asked me a lot of questions he wanted to put in the paper. Thing was that after he and I talked he saw a bunch of those people bringing things in and he talked to a whole lot of 'em. I dunno what he's gonna do with what he heard, but . . ." He let the sentence die off and relied on our imagination. Father got the threat and left us looking concerned.

By four-thirty when we locked up, the line had thinned out so that we could shut the doors without antagonizing anyone. Saylor came in and sat down wearily across the picnic table from me and we stared at each other for a bit. He had been so busy with the inundation that his usual cleaning and feeding routines were shot and the animals all resented it. He'd locked the cats into the outside cages and we could hear them roaring and coughing irritably from outside. Inside, the monkeys were storming around and the swirling—hungry—confusion sort of typified our problem. Two college kids who were drafted out of the swimming pool locker room came in and leaned against the side fence.

"He's gonna have to do something fast," Saylor said.

I knew he meant Father and though I didn't know exactly what had been done with everything I'd taken in, I could picture the mess that must be spread around the zoo.

"Yeah," I said. "What's the biggest problem?"

Saylor began waving his arms and sputtering as if he didn't know where to start.

"It's . . . everything! There ain't no place to put anything anymore at all. We've got the floors covered all over. Things are piled on everything. You can't get feed to 'em or water and there's no place for nothin'! I've got birds stacked all the way around the inside of the shed and the floors covered with rabbits so every time I go in a half dozen leak out."

One of the locker boys broke in, "That little coon got out and ran under the Lion House and we didn't have time to go after him."

"I hope he'll be very happy," Saylor said bitterly. "The turtles and alligators were getting so thick I moved some of 'em into the crawl space under the outside cat cages and just boarded up the door. That's going to be some surprised coon."

"Will they hurt him?" I asked.

"No, he'll probably jump up on them pipes in there, but it'll keep him occupied till we can get to him. That's half the trouble, though. We've got so many things in separate boxes we can't take care of 'em, but we don't dare turn 'em in with each other for fear of somebody starting a fight."

"What do you mean?"

"Why, we don't have time to sex everything and if you'd get two or three male coyotes or peacocks or anything in with just one female, by the time you'd get back you're liable to find somebody all cut up or picked to death. Speaking of peacocks, I've got all the aisles in the Bird House stacked with cages and that bird we let in there keeps jumpin' back and forth on top of 'em and getting everybody stirred up."

Saylor snorted and struggled to his feet. "Now I've got to do something about those cats before the neighborhood starts complaining about the racket."

He started out the back door and the two boys hastily recalled they had been working since seven o'clock and they were on their own time. They disappeared in the direction of the bus stop. I could hear Saylor slamming the door to the refrigerator and struggling in the kitchen and I got a mental picture of him at the chopping block hacking horse meat while standing in a seething mass of guinea pigs and white mice. It seemed best to leave him alone. I gave a short thought to starting home myself, but I found I was so tired I couldn't face the effort and so just sat there staring around me.

Suddenly I noticed the tiny little money huddled against the front bars looking out at me with a soul-tearing plea. I jumped up and walked over, leaning across the guard rail to talk to him. Before I knew it, I was carrying on an inane conversation with him and he began to cheer up before my eyes. I was afraid to try to pet him, not knowing whether he'd bite or not, but we were doing splendidly when Father burst in carrying a crate of bruised lettuce heads. He set them down beside the door to the kitchen.

"We've got to leave a path in there. You can't walk across the floor. Come on, I'll take you home."

He walked toward the front door and prepared to let himself out with the snap lock. I suspected he was avoiding any possible conversation with Saylor whom he must have passed in the kitchen. I said good-by to my monkey and was pleased to see that he seemed quite happy even with my leaving as if he understood and was assured I'd be back. As we went out the door, Saylor came in pushing a cart full of meat chunks. Father and he nodded and we fled without a word.

On the way home in the car, I found out why the unusual farewell—so unlike Father's usual ebullience. "The *Eagle* called MacDonald for some follow-up stories on the new animals. It was the first he'd heard about it and he wants to see me tomorrow. He wants to know where the money is coming from to feed them, he wants to be assured that they are all getting proper care, and he wants to know if I think it is appropriate for the City to be assuming responsibility for all this private property. At least he gave me all night to think of the answers."

# 3

## *Mostly Alligators*

By the time I awoke the following morning, Father had already gone. It was only a little after seven, but he had clearly headed out early. I asked if he'd left any instructions for me, but Mother said he hadn't said much of anything. It'd never really cooled down during the night and the thermometer on the back screen read ninety with the sun still hidden behind the garage. Mother said that Father had not slept well. I doubted if it was the heat.

After a light, slow breakfast I wandered out on to the front porch swing to try to plan my day. I got it creaking back and forth properly, but as usual this made me feel like I was going to pitch out on the back swing, so I got it stopped and shoved it longways and this was much better. I lay down on its length and as it rose and fell I tried to decide how to invest my energies.

I found myself torn between two programs. The heat and my general laziness urged that I take the latest P. G. Wodehouse borrowed from the library and get down into the basement between my two fans. On the other hand I have always hated to see something left unresolved and I found myself curious and unsatisfied about what was going on at the zoo. The thought of the struggle it'd take to get to the park kept me from moving, and the feeling that something was going on behind my back kept me out of the basement.

I decided to temporize and read the paper. No one had brought it in and I could see it lying on the sidewalk out front. I rolled off the swing, got the thing, and climbed back on without interrupting the stroke. Working from the back, I read the comics, checked the movie page, and was about to drop the second section on the floor when its front page caught me with sickening recognition. Across the top it read as usual: Home Town News. Beneath it were six pictures artfully distributed around the page in the *Eagle*'s best feature style. Here was a line of people standing outside the Lion House with pets dangling from various hands. There was a sullen child with a pet rabbit peering over the Niagara Falls on a Shredded Wheat box. And so it went around the page, each picture with a fat caption below milking all the human interest they could get out of it, but reminding every literate citizen of the surplus animal program.

I stumbled off the swing and into the house and after giving Mother a flying report changed into a respectable set of slacks and sport shirt and headed for the bus.

By the time I made the park, I was running a full half hour behind my arrival the day before and I visualized a mob swirling at the gates. I eased past the spot where the goat had been and found him gone, so I took off down the street as briskly as possible in the heat. By the time I got to the Lion House, I could see there was a cluster of cars parked out front, but no line. The cats had been locked out in their outdoor cages and the front doors were open, so I went in the public entrance, avoiding the floor-ful of mice, turtles, and whatever behind. Saylor was back at the picnic table surrounded by half a dozen citizens.

"Well it's about time," he shouted at me. "Your dad's give me two days' worth of orders and I can't even get started. You going to take over here?"

"Whatever you say. Nobody'd told me anything and if I hadn't seen the *Eagle* I wouldn't be here now. How can I help?"

Between us we absorbed one canary, two vegetable crates with a ringneck pheasant cock in each, one wing-shot mallard, and a two-foot-long Florida "alligator." With these accepted, recorded, and thanks duly expressed, there was a lull. Either we'd finally drained off the city's surplus, or the morning's story was still too fresh for the first wave to hit us. I went over and saluted my little monkey who was hanging on the bars half-way up the cage, clearly delighted to see me.

"Has this little guy eaten anything, Mr. Saylor?"

"I don't have time to watch. I threw him some lettuce leaves and a handful of peanuts. Don't know whether he's taken any or not."

There were some peanut shells strewn about and some of the lettuce had been nibbled on, so I felt better. There was also half an apple on the floor.

"Did you give him that apple or did someone throw it in?"

"Neither. It's from the baboons. I dunno whether they gave it to him or they were fighting and it rolled through the bars."

"What kind of a monkey is he?"

"All I know is he ain't like the others." I'd forgotten that Saylor never claimed to be a zoologist.

"Did you see my father?"

"Yeah, he was in early. He's got all kinds of plans. We're supposed to spend the day getting things sorted out. He's got a bunch of packing boxes out back and there's a pair of so-called carpenters from the shops puttin' wire across the fronts and making little doors for feedin'. I'm supposed to collect all the same kinds of birds I can find and put 'em together. He's got an idea for the squirrels that may work, though. They're making him a bunch of feeding platforms that he's going to put up out in the park and then we're supposed to turn the squirrels loose. He told me to pick out the best turtles and take the rest up on the river north of town. He wants something done about the alligators, too. Anyway I gotta get busy."

The day proceeded to shake out and by noon I began to think we might make it. I kept one eye on the picnic table and whenever someone would appear carrying something, I'd head back, but we probably didn't get a dozen specimens by lunch time. The rest of the time I drifted from one reorganization operation to another.

As Saylor said, the squirrels went quickly. Until Father could get overhead feeding shelves built, Saylor temporized by piling wooden boxes up to six or eight feet and putting a sheet iron feeding tray on top. Saylor would fill these trays with soybeans and chicken feed (and later with nuts the WPA men raked up from some of the parks which had walnut and hazelnut trees) and then he would lug the boxes of squirrels up a step ladder to the top of the platforms. He'd pry a corner loose on each 'cage' and the squirrels would burst out of the opening, shoot across the trays in a spray of grain and jump for the nearest branch. They'd scamper up high enough to consider the scene and then they'd look back at the food and scold and generally unburden themselves on their recent treatment. By the time Bob would be back in the building to get another armload of boxes, most of the last batch would be back down on the trays, putting away food as if they'd been there all their lives.

In the weeks to come, Saylor and Jim probably turned a hundred or so loose in this way, and the trees in the zoo park must have absorbed half of these. The rest spread out through town. The most remarkable thing about the squirrel receipt was the apparent relationship between the abandoned pets and their former owners. For months after the original delivery, the families would visit the zoo on weekends, and the squirrels would come down out of the trees to greet them. There'd be great chattering and scampering and the pets would nibble food from the owners' hands—but never let themselves be touched. There appeared to be a new reserve. Squirrels which had previously sat on shoulders and explored pockets would now eat from hands, but only if the animal could keep one foot on a park bench or the sidewalk. Saylor, who was rarely seduced by the romantic, was convinced we had a park full of frauds. He maintained bitterly that "them squirrels'll welcome anybody that's got his hand out." The owners were equally convinced it was "their" squirrels who were coming down —and Saylor couldn't prove it wasn't.

The turtle deluge—which was mostly made of terrapins —drained off nicely. Saylor sorted them into slow-moving heaps until he'd picked out about fifteen that were either the largest or had the most colorful shells. He stored these in washtubs under the sink, for the present, and then loaded the forty or fifty left over into the back of the park pick-up truck. At the same time, he culled out the seediest looking possums and coons (which still left plenty for potential displays if Father could ever find the space) and shoved them into the truck in the boxes they came in. This required scraping a few dozen turtles to one side to clear a corner in the truck bed, but ultimately everybody got right side up and Saylor rolled out.

When he got back from his expedition, he reported he'd driven up north of Valley Center along the Little Arkansas and Chisholm Creek, and whenever the streams would make a bend toward the road he'd pull over and sow some wildlife. By dint of liberating a couple of animals and six or eight terrapins every half mile through the bottom land, he managed to clear the truck and was back within an hour, ready to face up to the great experiment. He and Father had decided to amalgamate the alligators, regardless of age or size.

The question of the hour was: would the five huge alligators in the pit consider the twenty-some little ones we'd gotten—lunch?

The alligator pit was one of the few exhibits in our zoo that was a total success. It was a typical zoo fixture designed with an island in the center surrounded by a concrete, water-filled moat, and it was a sublime example of perfect zoomanship: a high-level attraction with next to no upkeep required. The island was about thirty feet across and sort of crowned out of clay and sand which eased down to the water level all the way around. The water was properly green and filthy and was about five feet wide and shoulder deep—if anybody had fallen in. The whole thing was surrounded by a waist-high stone fence on the outside which was just high enough to keep kids from toppling over and low enough that a man full of a Sunday picnic could lean across it in comfort.

Father had inherited five simply enormous alligators in this thing. They were all about the same size with the smallest some ten or twelve feet long and weighing about 500 pounds, and they would lie out in the center of that island for weeks, indeed months, at a time. About once an hour one of them would move a leg or a tail and this would generate a great uproar of "Look, Mom, look!" and by the time everyone got there, total paralysis would have set in again. On a really hot day sometimes as many as two of the beasts would begin to stir and gradually get up enough momentum to slide down into the water. They'd lie there with just the tips of their snouts out and then in a couple of hours they'd struggle back on to the land to bake again. If you managed to hit a day with really furious activity going, you could see this sequence as much as once every four hours. The rest of the time they did absolutely nothing.

In spite of this, there was always a rim of people hanging over the parapet. And they all seemed to react in the same way. The adults would stare at each one of the beasts, trying to see if they really were alive. Once they'd satisfied themselves that they had actually seen one breathe if only with the tiniest inflation or if they could see a black eye showing through a slit, the spectator would go motionless himself and just stare. All emotion would drain away and in no time at all he would have joined the rest of the grownups staring dead-pan down into the pit. Every so often you'd see a parent shake loose from his trance and turn slowly around to see if the kids were still in the neighborhood.

The kids came and went with great turnover. One of them would roar up and stare down and then take one of two courses of action. Either he'd pivot in disgust and dash off somewhere else, or he'd start looking around for something to throw. This would turn out to be a piece of gravel or a peanut or a crumpled popcorn sack and he'd fire it over the side at one of the alligators. About half the time he'd hit his target and the missile would bounce off its tough hide without making the faintest bit of difference. I never once saw any reaction of any kind. The kid would try this a couple more times and then shear off in disgust.

So far as the zoo was concerned, it had three levels of response to this treatment. First, there was a faded sign leaning slightly off center out in the middle of the island which read, "Do Not Throw Anything In This Exhibit." Then Saylor saw to it there was never anything of much size like bottles or rocks left near the pit. And finally, about twice during the week and once a day on weekends, Jim would screw a pressure hose on to a spigot by the sidewalk and he'd blast the whole island with water, sluicing it down from the center out. This would float the debris into the moat where it would either sink or float over to the screen-covered drainpipe. When he got everything drifted into one place, he'd seine it out with a long-handled dip net and the cleaning would be finished. The water would wash the accumulated dust off the alligators and for a few moments make them look as near to life as they ever got.

The beasts got fed twice a week whether they needed it or not. This amounted to about 25 pounds of very dead fish heaved over the side onto the island. Occasionally you could see one eat something. Usually not, but the stuff seemed to disappear some way and the 'gators had managed to live at least 20 years that we knew of.

So far as I was concerned, the most astonishing aspect of the alligator pit was their hibernation. The year before, during our first Thanksgiving in Wichita, I'd gone over to the zoo for a quick look with Father. Wichita usually got cold and raw very quickly after Hallow'een and by Thanksgiving there were some hard frosts and the ground was dry and brittle. We'd stopped off for Father to see how everything was taking the cold and had found Jim and Saylor beside the alligator pit. The zoo's one old truck had been driven up on the sidewalk and its open bed had five huge planks in the back. The planks had been painters' scaffolds and showed the spatterings of years of park green and gray. Beside the half-ton truck there was one of the big Park Department work trucks with an A-shaped crane mounted on the back.

"What are you doing?" Father had asked.

"Puttin' the 'gators away."

Father had looked into the pit and could see the reptiles covered with dust, looking as if they hadn't moved for weeks.

"Haven't moved for a couple of weeks," Saylor said, "so I think they're ready. I called the barns and they sent out a truck."

"What's the boom for?"

"*They* use it for settin' creosote logs on the parkways. We use it for hoistin' 'gators."

Saylor and the truckmen had obviously done this before, and without much conversation they rigged a heavy rope and made a loop in the end. Saylor stood in the loop and the crane lifted him up and over the moat and lowered him down onto the island. Jim then threw him a loose piece of rope that had been tied into a long figure-eight and he picked it up and carried it to the nearest 'gator. He kicked him casually and got no response so he lifted his snout and slipped one loop of the rope over his head and jerked it back till it caught on the forelegs. He then pulled the loops out as long as they'd go and just got the other one over the tail. Once he'd pulled this back up to the rear legs, he caught the boom rope and tied it at the center of the figure-eight.

"OK. Take 'im up," he shouted across at the truck driver. Then, as we watched in amazement, they lifted the 'gator into the air. He sagged appreciably in the middle, but gave no sign whatever of life. He sailed out over the moat and the parapet and, as they turned the truck, was lowered carefully onto one of the painters' planks. The smaller truck creaked and settled down on its springs. Jim struggled the rope off of him and left him there, lying astride the plank with his legs hanging down each side.

"Come on. Get the rope back."

They proceeded to get another one up and over and eased it beside the first. This so taxed the truck it was plain they were going to have to unload the pair before going on with the others.

"What are you going to do with them?" Father asked, intrigued.

"Put 'em under the Lion House."

So we watched the two trucks drive down the sidewalks to the rear of the Lion House and here they backed up to the entrances to the crawl spaces under the inside floor. By means of a great deal of prying and heaving they lifted a loaded plank at a time off the truck and down onto rollers and then slid them under the building.

While the trucks were driving back to the pit for the next load Father said, "I gather they've hibernated."

"Yeah, they're dead as doornails. They begin to freeze up in late October and by now they're completely gone. I try to get 'em out before the first snow, but there's been some years when I ain't quite made it and it didn't seem to hurt 'em any."

"When do you put them back?"

"Oh, I try to get'em out 'bout Easter." A big grin began to spread over his face. "You gotta be careful you don't wait too long in the spring, though. Anybody tell you about the big snow year before last?"

Father couldn't remember anyone had.

" 'Bout February we had one helluva blizzard. Started the week before George Washington's Birthday and it snowed some for ten days running. Stayed below zero all during the storm and we couldn't keep the heat up in the buildings. Got down to the forties in the Bird House and we were afraid we'd chill the monkeys in the Lion House so we kept the heat up full blast night and day.

" 'Bout the middle of the second week we began to hear funny noises in the refrigerator in the back room and then Jim claimed he saw the radiators jump around. I give him a hard time till I noticed the spigots in the kitchen seemed to be jerkin' up and down.

"Finally figured out what was happening. The steam pipes down under the floor'd been going so high for so long that the crawl space got all heated up and it thawed out those damn alligators. When they come to they were four months hungry and they began to squirm around, and when they'd swing their tails they'd bang up against the pipes and jar all the plumbing!" Saylor got red in the face and wheezed as he told this and came as close to laughing as I ever saw him.

"What'd you do?" Father wanted to know.

"Oh, we had a helluva time trying to decide. If we cooled the space down, we'd thin out the steam and we needed everything we could get upstairs. But we were 'fraid they'd bust something if we let 'em rip and then we'd have to go down under there to fix it. Finally sort of split the difference. I opened some vents under the outside cat cages and that cooled things off enough to make the 'gators sluggish and then when we quit pouring heat through the pipes after the storm quit, they finally conked out wherever they was at. When we went in to get 'em in March, they was all over the place. I remember we had to put ropes around 'em and pull 'em out through the hole with a winch. I hope we never get stuck with that one again!"

All this came to mind on this breathless August afternoon when it strained the brain to think it would ever cool down enough to freeze anything again. The question at hand was what to do with two dozen, two- and three-foot long, very active young alligators. They took up a major part of the zoo's kitchen floor. They were squirming around, climbing on top of each other, threatening to climb over the wooden planks we'd propped up for walls, and clearly were as hungry and frisky as the five monsters out in the pit were lethargic. There was no way to keep water in with them and we'd all heard stories which implied they had to have moisture to cover their skin and certainly to get the hamburger down.

Father had peremptorily ordered Saylor to "get 'em out

of the kitchen and throw the whole lot in with the big ones." In the confusion of all the other surplus, it sounded like a forthright decision, but when the time came to move them, we all stood around in flat silence.

"Lively little rascals, ain't they?" Saylor finally remarked. All of them had their heads up with the beady little eyes looking from one to the other of us, expecting something edible.

"Are they fast enough to get away if one of the big ones started after them?" I asked.

Nobody said anything, and then one of the lifeguards from Linwood Park who'd been drafted for the afternoon said, "Trouble is, they might just walk in front of one of the big devils and all he'd have to do is snap 'em up."

We stared a while and Saylor said, "Don't suppose I'd dare turn 'em loose up on the river, huh?"

I promptly got mental pictures of two English sparrows introduced and soon spreading like wildfire, of six starlings multiplying across a continent—and tiny alligators breeding up the prairie tributaries and spreading across the plains by the thousands, driving the jack rabbits into the hills.

"No," I said.

"Then let's throw 'em over and see what happens." Saylor waited for someone to dissuade him, and getting no response, walked to a closet and pulled two thick leather gloves down from the shelf. "Wonder if you can catch 'em?" he muttered to himself as he surveyed the group.

All of the youngsters were looking up at him now, and he picked out the closest who was also the largest. He cautiously reached toward him, but the little beast made no sign of moving, and when Saylor grabbed for him, catching him over the front legs and behind the head, he didn't twitch a muscle. Saylor lifted him up at arm's length and he hung down like a fat, leather belt.

Bob started out the door and we all followed in silence as if the animal were about to be interred. When we got to the alligator pit, he dislodged a pair of stupefied citizens and stood there by the railing, holding the little one out in front of him over the moat. He looked from one of us to the other, and we all hastily looked across at the big five, lying out there in the hot dust, as quiet as ever.

"Well, here goes nothing," he said, and swung the 'gator in a wide arc and flung him across to the island. He landed with a thud and his head snapped up to see where he was. We stepped to the stone parapet and watched intently. The little guy suddenly darted up the hill, ran across two of the big ones and then, apparently to see better where he was, ran up on the head of the big one on top of the hill.

The big one opened an eye slowly, looked deliberately down his snout—and closed it again. Complete anti-climax! He couldn't have cared less.

Reassured, we all rushed back and began scooping the things up with both hands and flinging them over the side. In ten minutes we had reclaimed their corner of the kitchen and Jim was sluicing down the area with one hand, while trying to keep the spray off the rabbits and white mice with a broom in the other.

The first steps at organization had gone with a snap. We congratulated ourselves and took on a knowledgeable, professional air. This zoo business was clearly overrated. Anyone with a little common sense could cope with anything. And indeed had the whole operation gone as simply as the reptilian disposal, it would have been a grand success. Turtles, terrapins, and "alligators" (we later found out the things were caymans which never get longer than three or four feet, and inconveniently, never grow sluggish in winter!), all neatly absorbed or disposed of. We proceeded with renewed hope—dwelling in a false euphoria.

# 4

# *Discord*

Father, in the meantime, had reported to the Director of Parks.

Alfred MacDonald had never understood the need for easing a situation. He had never really given it any thought, but the idea of a "good team, all working toward a common goal" simply had never crossed his mind. He knew he was in charge of the Park Department, and he knew he had three supervisors under him. Jack Magathan was Chief Forester, and he was responsible for the plantings. Charlie Peterson was in charge of security, and if there had been a park police force, he would have been its captain. (As it was there was only himself and one police car—obligated to patrol some thirty parks, miles of roadways, and flush out necking couples from spots the mind of man knoweth not where.) And Bernie Goodrum, Director of Recreation. Assigned to Magathan and Goodrum were a hundred and fifty-some others, but they all worked for MacDonald, and if they didn't know it or like it there were plenty of others who could use the job.

Technically—and the weekly staff meeting of the three supervisors perpetuated the myth—MacDonald "told" the three division heads, and they then ran their sections. In fact, in MacDonald's eyes, *everybody* worked for him and him alone. The heads could carry messages and make suggestions, but there was never a geranium planted nor a grass-green watered that MacDonald did not know about personally and which was planted and watered, in MacDonald's mind, because MacDonald wanted it so.

Never before had he found out something about one of his parks by reading it in the newspaper. And he was apoplectic.

Father timed his rival at the Park Board offices to the second of his appointment, threw the big hand to the accumulated secretaries, and breezed into the Director's office already talking. "Mr. MacDonald! Have you heard what's happening at the zoo! It's tremendous! Some way people heard about that pelican we got and it's produced the most amazing collection of display material you've ever seen. I tell you we're getting hundreds of dollars worth of really valuable exhibits for absolutely nothing, and we're rendering a real service to the community. People are bringing in the most adorable little things—and people are hearing about the parks for the first time. It's fantastic publicity and it isn't costing us . . ."

"Where are you putting these valuable acquisitions?"

"My gosh, we've got 'em everywhere! We've got coyotes in the pheasant pens, and we've got guinea pigs behind the refrigerator and we've got . . ."

"Why would you want guinea pigs at all?"

"Well, once we get a chance to fix things up, we can do a really beautiful series of rodent displays. We can show the children the various kinds which make appealing pets—white mice and white rats and hamsters, and then we can trace the small indigenous mammalia—we've got possums and coons and a muskrat and skunks and . . ."

"How many guinea pigs do you have?"

"Well, there are quite a number right now, and we'll want to thin these down somewhat, but . . ."

"Precisely how many?"

"Well, it isn't a stable population, of course, but I suspect we have three or four dozen, maybe."

"You don't expect to keep all of them?"

"Oh my no, what I thought . . ."

"Are you aware that in accepting these animals you are making them municipal property and are responsible for their care and preservation?"

"Oh, we're taking good care of them, they're just temporarily . . ."

"And as municipal property they cannot be sold without being placed for public auction, that they cannot be given away without antagonizing the local pet stores and dislocating their markets, and they cannot be destroyed without exhibiting bad faith to the donors who will expect to find them on display? Are you aware you have committed the honor of the city and of myself without taking anyone into your confidence?"

Father's offensive was lost, and so were his easy answers.

"I assume that the other species are accumulating in the same magnitude as the guinea pigs?"

"Well, no, there are more of them than most . . ."

"Then what are all these things being fed with?"

"We're getting a lot of cuttings that are discarded in the supermarkets."

"Presumably that accounts for your greens eaters. Where is the meat coming from and the seed and feed? You must know that the zoo rations are figured and budgeted a year ahead. Presumably you are now feeding rations you will need next May and June?"

Father acted like this was meant to be rhetorical, and tried to shift the conversation from the specific to the general.

"You see, Mr. MacDonald, what I'm hoping we can do is . . ." a sudden idea struck him that had only just entered his mind and he swept off inspired, "use this material for trading purposes! We can take this surplus stock and trade it to other zoos and municipalities for materials we need. And we can use WPA labor to work up inexpensive display areas which will give people something to look at when they come out to the parks." He had it now. "One of the most distressing things to me about the magnificent plantings and floral displays in Riverside has been that too many people just drive through—the Sunday outing in the car—they don't get out and walk around and see what you've done there. If we give them reasons to stop and picnic and see a zoo whose displays have variety and breadth and spread through the park we'll double the use. Here's an opportunity to commit the service clubs . . . the church groups . . . some of the people in Eastborough to the kind of thing you're doing. We've got an opportunity here to put Wichita on the map for a very minimum of money and a lot of imagination. We can have the finest zoological display between St. Louis and Denver here. We can do it with the resources we have already. It'll sell itself if we just give it a chance. It's educational. It's wholesome recreation. It will engage the business community and they'll recognize it as appealing to the trade area. It can symbolize your own idea of a park system made equally of beauty and usefulness."

MacDonald's expression never changed. He looked back at Father and said without expression, "You will close the park at once, place signs at the gates that no further animals will be accepted beginning immediately. In the meantime, I want those extra animals housed in such a way that we can receive no criticism for their health or comfort. Perhaps together we can decide what can be done with them after that."

Father looked discomfited and failed to respond with the ready agreement that MacDonald expected.

"What's the matter?", the Director asked.

"Well, sir," Father replied somewhat diffidently, "I think we've got to recognize that we've already gone somewhat beyond that. You see, the newspapers are interested in the thing now, and any step like closing down the zoo and things like that . . . well, I can see pictures of a little girl holding up her bunny beside a "zoo closed sign". . . . Too, we're rendering the community a service in assisting them with their pets. What I mean is, a zoo will foster the love of children for animals, but it must also accept some of the responsibility for . . ."

"What do you mean a picture of a little girl and her . . . her rabbit?"

"Well, you know how these stories get written. Picture of a tear-stained child who wanted to share her pet with all the other children of Wichita. City Hall slams the door in her face. Is this what we're paying taxes for? Questions to the City Manager. You know, that sort of thing. These newspapers are absolutely ruthless if they get off on the wrong foot. I think . . ."

MacDonald's face showed he was appalled at the lengths to which this thing could take him. Years of careful work fostering sympathetic, even enthusiastic support of his park program, threatened with a lunatic stunt like this . . . this . . . the potential enormity of the disaster, shattering two decades of well-ordered administration. His mind boggled at the prospect.

"Very well," he said, trying to keep himself under control. "I will expect you to conclude this in such a way that not one word of criticism is heard in any quarter. I want this resolved and resolved quickly. And I trust you understand that I do not want anything, anything, like this ever to happen again. Do we understand each other?"

"Yes, sir. I think I see what you're driving at, and I'll get right on it."

Father pivoted and fled.

# 5

# *Resolution*

Father arrived at the Lion House quiet.

Father had always been limited to three speeds: brisk, ebullient, and mad. In all my life, I'd never seen him depressed or pessimistic. When things were going badly for him, he would burst into righteous wrath and clothe himself in the fury of the wronged. The secret was to know which way he was going to go, and with a teen-ager's experience, I knew the best thing to do was lie low until I found where we were headed. His present mood was without precedent. I faded behind a guard rail and scratched the ears on my little monkey while the situation resolved itself.

"Bob," he said, "get everybody together. We've got to have a council of war."

Saylor went out the door and Father walked back and forth absently staring at the cat cages and pulling his nose.

By the time Saylor returned with the loaned lifeguards, Jim, and the two carpenters from the park barns, it was four-thirty and time to lock up for the day. Saylor nudged the last visitors out the door, shot the bolt, and pulled the "Closed" blinds down.

The men drifted over to the corner in front of the black leopards and leaned against the guard rail. Father convened the meeting with a detailed report of his moments with MacDonald.

"So there's where we stand at City Hall. Now let me get the picture here. How much came in today?"

" 'Bout a dozen things. Got a good, wing-shot Canadian goose. Got another 'coon, looks in good shape. Got a little green parrot. Rest of the stuff was routine," Saylor reported.

"How much have you cleared out?"

He heard a quick review of the squirrel, turtle, and alligator situation.

"Um. What MacDonald doesn't find out won't hurt him. Good job, Bob. Forgetting the rabbits and mice, how many small animals have we got?"

"Probably a hundred or so."

"Okay. Let's talk about the Bird House. Is it leaking any?"

"Air or water?"

"Either one."

"If you mean air, we've got all the top sashes open and

it's hotter'n Hades up high in there. If you was to close 'em for fall weather, though, they'd leak cold like crazy. Half the putty's shot and it comes in around the panes."

"And water?" Father asked.

"Nope, it's pretty tight against rain and snow."

"How did it heat the last few weeks of the spring?"

"Lousy. It's hot as blazes around the radiators and it feels like ice across the floor and up in the big flight cage."

I was baffled at where Father could be heading. The Bird House was as near to nothing as anything in the park. The Lion House had style, the bear pits (which apparently were designed by the architect who did Leavenworth) at least had permanence, but the Bird House was an absolute disaster. As far as exhibits went, it consisted of a central flight cage about the size of a single tennis court (some twenty-five feet high), and a batch of eight-foot, individual display cages down each side. At a distance the thing was hidden by the trees, and looked fairly respectable. Up close its antecedents were showing. Apparently the money had run out about half way along, and someone appeared to have found a huge collection of surplus schoolhouse windows at just the moment of need. They had taken these windows and stood them on top of each other like a house of cards until the whole thing was big enough to cover the cages inside. At this point they put on a flat roof, painted everything that wasn't glass a grimy green, and moved out. The result was one of the lightest bird houses in the business, but one that leaked air all winter and collected it all summer. It was impossible to keep clean, and was hung together with two-by-fours like some Japanese teahouse made to be burned at the end of the festival.

"That's what I expected," Father was saying. "Now let me try something and see how it sounds. We've got to get the animals out of all these boxes and fast. What if we cleared the Bird House completely, and moved everything that's in it plus everything new we've got with feathers on it, and set up flight cages at my home? That would clear the present cages here. How many are there, by the way?"

Saylor looked puzzled and everyone turned to Jim.

"You got the big cage in the middle, Mister Bernie, and you got six cages down each side. They's off the ground two foot, y'know."

"Fine. Suppose we used all these for the small animals—'coons, possums, coyotes, the fox, skunks, the badgers—that it? Have I left anything out?"

"You got a crummy-looking porcupine in there. Smells terrible, too."

"Okay, porcupines. Could these be distributed into those twelve cages so you didn't have to mix species? And would they fight? Could you get away with it?"

Everybody looked at Saylor. "It'd depend on how many you had of which. If you had one male and six females or the other way around, they'd probably kill each other off, but I 'spect things are pretty well mixed up. It might work."

"Good. Now, if we, say, cut the big cage up into four or five enclosures, and put in two pot-bellied stoves to back up the steam, could we keep the place warm enough?"

Jim and Saylor looked at each other and nodded slowly.

"All right," Father concluded. "Is there anything wrong with the idea, then, of using the Bird House for the small stuff until we can get things sorted out?"

"Yeah," said Saylor. "What about the rats?"

Father started to say he wasn't interested in the white rats and mice right then, but he caught himself. "Oh, you mean the vermin in the Bird House. Yes, I'd forgotten that. Is it getting worse, or about the same?"

"Well, right now," Saylor replied, "it's actually better'n usual. Most everything is livin' outside now'n the summer. Peterson said he got two or three over the weekend, and I saw one last night, but they're pretty well under control. It's the cold weather that'll bring 'em in."

This whole thing was a bizarre situation that had astonished me the winter before. Shortly before we'd moved to Wichita, the *Saturday Evening Post* had run a cartoon which showed two dowagers in a zoo house, and the artist had drawn little squiggles up from each cage. The caption read, "Heavens, Agatha, think what the jungle must smell like!" This had struck me as hilarious at the time and had stuck in my mind.

I was therefore pleasantly surprised when Father had gotten mixed up with the zoo and I had suddenly become conscious of how zoos were run, to find that there was almost no odor of any kind in the Wichita buildings except for a pleasant cedar perfume left from the floor sweepings. Noticing the cleanliness apparent everywhere, and knowing that the zoo had had almost no illness for years past, I was amazed to hear Father say that *at night* the Bird House and the bear pens were alive with rats. This repellent piece of news turned up because Charlie Peterson, the park policeman, had asked Father if he wanted to come out with him and shoot a few?

It developed that every few nights during his pre-midnight check of the zoo properties, he would take a five-cell torch from the patrol car, use his night keys to get into the Bird House, and unlimber his revolver. He'd sweep the floor with the flashlight, and when it would pick up a pair of beady eyes, he would blast away. It soon became apparent that in this way his marksmanship with a hand gun was probably faster and better than that of anyone in the regular police department.

He had asked Father if he'd like to come over for an hour and get in a little practice. Father, who hadn't used a side arm since his World War I days, had declined the revolver, but he'd taken our target rifle and joined him. Mother was terrified at the whole arrangement and was certain they were going to shoot each other, but Father sailed off into the night.

The next morning we got the report that in deference to his lack of practice, instead of roaming around and firing from the hip, they had taken up positions on two boxes out in the middle of the main cage and sat there in the dark. The birds were all asleep on perches around the place, and the street lights coming through the glass walls lit things up fairly well, once their eyes got accustomed to the gloom. Sure enough, the outside lights picked up the eyes of something coming up out of a hole. Father sighted down the rifle and fired away. Apparently he hit the rat right where he intended to, and rolled him about a foot across the floor, stone dead. The explosion of the gun, though, blasted off all the birds and there was bedlam in the place. In the dark, some of the birds fell off the perches and couldn't find their way back, others flew into the wire, much shrieking and flapping about, and it took a full ten minutes for the place to settle down again. About this time another rat appeared on Peterson's side, and the whole routine was run through again. Apparently they kept it up till they'd gotten a dozen or so of the things, and finally went home, leaving a building full of birds with bags under their eyes. Jim would check each morning to see if Peterson had been there the night before, and if so, carry off the results of the action.

I found it hard enough to believe that they even had the rats, but it was even stranger that no one ever saw one around during the daytime. Further, I'd always heard that rats were so intelligent that they never made the same mistake twice. If so, the communication of the colony must have been lousy, because they kept coming out of those holes and Peterson kept knocking them off night after night, month after month. I would have thought the noise alone would have been enough to bring on trauma, but they appeared impervious and must have stood in line to come out of the holes.

"I think we can get away with it," Father ventured, "if we really load the runways with poison, and drill some holes in the floorboards so we can drop pellets underneath. Don't you think that'll hold them off, Bob?"

"It oughta. Don't know, though. The birds were always up on their perches at night, so it never made no difference what happened on the floor. Come to think of it, though, I'm not so sure it'd make much difference to what you're talking about anyway. The coyotes and the fox'd probably eat anything that showed its head. Possums'n 'coons'd sleep on a shelf. Don't know what'd happen to the skunks, but they ought to be able to take care of themselves. I think you might get away with it. What're you going to do with the rabbits and things?"

"I think I've got an idea there. MacDonald says they're municipal property, so I think I can just keep them on city land. Can you think of any reason why they can't be given to the Crippled Children's Home and the Florence Crittenden Home? I think I'll make a few calls."

He turned to the carpenters. "Okay, let's try it. Tomorrow morning see if you can tear down a mess of those packing boxes and put 'em together as flight cages. We'll need six or eight about two feet deep, three feet wide, and maybe three or four feet high. Try to make them uniform so we can stack them on top of each other against the wall in my garage. There're scraps of hardware cloth out in the shed you can use for the fronts. We can slip newspaper up inside and make cleaning easier.

"Jim, you and the boys here can start working on the Bird House. Cover any wooden posts with wire up to head high so no one can gnaw out, and have her ready when we move the birds. Bob, you'll have your hands full taking care of everything in the meantime. With this heat we've got to be especially careful not to let anything go dry, and don't neglect the cats and monkeys. We can't let the routine care slip. I know it means everyone working faster and longer, but if we bring this off, we can come up with a zoo we can really be proud of, and you and Jim will have a ten-man staff under each of you! Let's get the late feeding started now, I'll keep Chuck here for a week or so to take care of anything new people bring in, and let's try to get it all stabilized by the end of the week. OK? Let's roll."

And that was how my mother inherited a bird farm in one of Wichita's "better residential districts"—to her despair and mortification.

My mother was the daughter of a very dignified Congregational minister, and she had married Father when both of them had been young schoolteachers. As Father had gone up the professional ladder, she had played the role of the schoolteacher's wife (in the Twenties in Kansas, a female teacher could not smoke, play cards, be a Catholic, or marry; she had blown the latter and was retired at the end of the semester) and she filled the role very nicely. By the time Father became a department head, she was entertaining graciously and was a member of all the proper church groups. When we got to Wichita, she had picked out a nice, middle-class home on College Hill and added the fashionable Art and Literature Club to her activities. The manager of the leading dry-goods store lived with his family to the right of us, the head of the local Bell Telephone Company and family were to the left, and no less than two doctors' families lived across the street. My closest friend was the son of the head of the Veterans Administration Hospital, and while Mother had no desire to rise any higher in the local social ladder, she was completely comfortable where she was and had expected to remain there. When Father apprised her of the imminence of three hundred birds, her first thought was, "What will the neighbors think!"

Father's view was, "What the hell difference does it make?" and my thought was, so long as I wasn't expected to look after them it had a certain amount of dramatic interest.

In the ensuing days, the park truck would drive up, back down the driveway to the garage, unload three or four of the new cages, and drive away. Mother would watch from the screened-in back porch and look up and down the back yards to see if anyone was noticing what was going on. Father and Saylor worked out a bird census of the stock they had on hand, and then divided it up on paper so that each cage would have birds of like size if not necessarily similar species, and which would eat the same food. Again depending on size and habit, they distributed the specimens into the proper spaces. While you could only put two or three cockatoos together, you could put a couple dozen canaries in one cage and six or eight pairs of parakeets.

By the time they had everything on paper, it was clear they had underestimated the number of different enclosures they would need, and so the bulk overflowed the garage and many had to be set up on the back porch. Mother carefully kept the green-slatted blinds rolled down on the porch so no one could see in, and she made Father promise that he would keep the "noisy" birds in the garage.

By the end of the week, all the cages were ready, and the transfer of the material began. The newly acquired pets moved quickly and easily since the majority of them were still either in their own cages as when acquired, or they'd been put into portable temporary cages, but the regular stock from the Bird House was another thing. It became a real struggle to catch the birds without either terrifying them till they hurt themselves, or run the risk of damaging them with the nets. The latter were two long-handled pieces of deep-sea fishing equipment that someone had brought back from Galveston. They worked reasonably well on big stock like parrots and macaws, but were next to worthless on the smaller birds.

Ultimately, Father remembered the rat-shooting episode, and recalled how helpless the birds had been in the dark. He and Saylor thus drew the obvious conclusion and abandoned the project till nightfall. At this point they moved into the Bird House with stepladders and proceeded to pick the specimens off perches like apples. The birds were easy to spot silhouetted against the glass windows, but there was still so little light they couldn't see the hands coming at them. This night transfer satisfied everybody. It was much faster for Father and the zoo men (the whole thing was cleared in two evenings), the birds never knew what hit them, and best of all, Mother saw the stuff deposited under cover of d. without the neighbors knowing.

Once everything was properly hidden behind the garage door or the green porch blinds, she felt much better. Thereafter, throughout the fall and winter until Father got his new building program going the next spring, Jim would drive over every morning and spend an hour cleaning and feeding, and drive off. Mother was always a bit nervous while the zoo truck was in the driveway, but none of the neighbors asked her any direct questions and she began to think she was going to get away with it all without any severe loss of standing.

I thought a garageful of exotic fowl was a great idea, and exploited the arrangement as far as I could push it once school started in the fall. I found it somewhat difficult to use at first, however. You couldn't be sure how the audience would react.

I was vigorously pursuing a tall, cultured young lady at the time with the unlikely name of Persis. She was the President of the Student Council and combined a straight "A" average with the most remarkable ability to fill a knitted sweater of anyone in the Senior Class. I had gotten from the talking-between-classes to the Coke-after-school stage, and I thought I could exploit the aviary as a teen-age version of the etchings gambit. I thus got her to come home with me after school, took her into the house, and casually remarked to my mother that I was going to take my guest out to the garage. The look of distress on Mother's face failed to deter me, and we sailed out through the porch's display and on into the major presentation in back.

I recall being conscious for the first time of something lacking in the ventilation of the garage, but I was casually going from cage to cage displaying great familiarity with the birds and giving her interesting facts not worth knowing about each species. When we came to one of the big macaws from the Kansas City theater, I reached over to scratch its craw and show her how affectionate the pets were. At the last moment, for some reason I changed my mind, and noticing that the young lady had a new yellow Ticonderoga pencil slid down in the notebook she was warming against that dramatic sweater, I reached over and pulled it out. I then casually ruffled the breast feathers of the macaw with the eraser end, giving her the knowing lecture the while. The macaw just as nonchalantly reached down and took the pencil in its beak and without the faintest effort sheared it into three pieces. The eraser end dropped to the floor. He shook the fragment that was the width of his beak free and dropped it, leaving me with the pointed stub. The cut end was sliced as smoothly as if it had been cut with a razor.

Someway the realization that that could just as easily have been my finger reduced my nonchalance, and Persis found a fast excuse for departure and fled. I later found out that her views on the expedition had produced the report, "They may be the world's rarest birds, but it smelled like a chicken farm to me."

I made considerably more points with my male friends on the menagerie, and usually brought home a couple after school each evening to show off the display. I found that the most popular exhibits were not the exotic tropical stuff, but the game birds that flowed through.

As soon as Father got things stabilized at the Zoo itself, the first improvements he made were for the pheasants, and thus they were the first to leave the garage and return to Riverside. As he had hinted, he convinced MacDonald that by using the WPA labor scattered around on various park projects, and by committing a minimum of money in wire and low-grade lumber, he could create a fairly spectacular row of outdoor pens. This was such a nominal sum that even MacDonald could absorb it, and thus the first rows of displays began to go up along the walks surrounding the Bird House. Once in place and painted a dark, park green, they did provide an unusual number of "stopping places" for a minimum of money.

At the beginning, Father moved out a flock of ringneck pheasants, and one good pair of goldens he'd gotten in the early days of the "dumping." He very carefully hung little signs listing the names of the donors of the material (the pelican man and the Canadian goose family were similarly immortalized at the duck pond), and the local hunters quickly got the idea.

The result was that as fast as he'd empty a cage in the garage, it'd be filled up until he could get a new pen at Riverside built. Thus the garage population stayed pretty much the same, while the zoo displays grew every week.

After the pheasants, came a clutter of wing-shot Chukar partridges from various sources, several "prairie chickens," and then a growing collection of live quail.

One of the most spectacular additions arrived in a slightly incongruous way. An oil rigger stopped by the zoo with a duck in a bucket and presented the whole thing to Saylor who called Father to say he thought he'd gotten a wood duck, but he couldn't be sure.

A wood duck is far and away the most spectacular member of the duck family, and not only are they valuable for their rarity, but everything about them is extraordinary. They have a dramatic crest on their heads, run as much as twenty inches long, with short necks and long tails, and they come in the most remarkable colors. Their topside is tastefully designed in glittering greens, blues, and purple, and the under-carriage is red, yellow, and white. Instead of centering on water with the usual duck approach to life, they prefer to live on nuts and insects back in the woods and build their nests in hollow trees—usually some 40 feet above the ground. The latter level puts the young in the position of the old elevator shaft joke, "The first step is a son-of-a-gun," but if they survive the push-off, nothing else is ever quite so bad.

When Father got to the zoo, he quickly saw why Saylor wasn't sure what he had. The bird had landed in an oil sump where they were draining a well, and was completely sodden with the mixture of oil, mud, and water that a sump collects. When the driller had scooped him out, he was literally sinking in the stuff, the petro-chemicals having cut the body oil off his feathers thus eliminating the surface tension that keeps a duck afloat. He was black and slimy with the stuff and trembling with cold and fear.

Thinking it too good to waste, Father grabbed the bucket and headed for home with it. Mother put up the traditional, "You're not going to bring that thing in the house, are you?" and Father as usual acted as if he hadn't heard it.

This was in the days before detergents and paper towels, so his conclusion that he had to get the slime off forced him to rolls of toilet paper, then washcloths and Lux soap flakes. He got the family dishpan out from under the sink and filled it with warm water from the tap and lifted the duck in. He was so sticky with the oil that he could barely flounder and could scarcely get his wings loose from his body. Father began laboriously stripping the oil off and throwing the paper in the wastebasket until he got down to the feathers themselves.

By this time the water was cold and the oil was congealing faster than ever. Father added more warm water and carried the pan over to the stove where he turned on two burners very low and set to work with the soap and the washcloths. The color of the feathers began to come up and just as things began to look hopeful, Mrs. Knightly, wife of the head of the English Department at the college, came in the back door with some dishes she had borrowed for a tea.

"My God!" she screamed. "You're cooking that duck alive!"

My mother almost fainted from embarrassment and swept her through the swinging door into the dining room, explaining wildly as she went.

The bird proved indeed to be a wood duck drake, and after a week in a box under the stove recovered in splendid style. Once it was wing-clipped, it was turned loose in the duck pond, whether it wanted to live by the water or not. The duck adapted immediately, and was one of the most attractive exhibits in the collection.

Similarly, Father came up with a sublime solution to the canary and parakeet problem which gave us a satisfaction out of all proportion to the predicament. In the course of his recreation programs, he had met a large number of elderly folks, some couples, but mostly widows living alone, who were almost penniless and who were living exclusively on tiny pension and relief checks. Because of their dependence on state and local funds, Father convinced MacDonald that they were in many respects wards of the municipality (and clearly no competition for the local pet market), so that it would be both fitting and proper to redistribute the songbirds among those aged who would promise to care for them.

This proved to be enormously successful, and the laboriously written letters of gratitude that Father received for months after this were almost too poignant to be endured. Anyone working with welfare cases learns the cliché that loneliness is the greatest curse of impoverished old age, but somehow these tiny birds dramatized what "loneliness" meant in a way that had never been real to any of us.

Apparently a live thing to talk to, or simply something to chirp a response, was magnified out of all proportion to what we would have believed. The simple act of caring for a bird—and knowing that the bird was dependent on the care-er—made the relationship important.

The mechanics of this distribution were carried out by the Welfare Department, and when they would find an elderly person who was appropriate and who asked for a bird, the welfare lady would call Saylor at the zoo, and he would have Jim bring whatever was involved down from the garage after the next morning's feeding. From our family's end, this meant that every few days another bird would disappear, and ultimately after a cage was emptied, one of the flight cages on the back porch could be moved to the garage. What these disappearances really meant was suddenly dramatized to me one evening when Father came in again, very late for supper.

He had a shaken, sort of absent look in his eyes, and he

reported that as he'd left City Hall at five-thirty he'd stopped in the Welfare Department to see how the program was going. Before he could see the appropriate staff member, he had had to wait for a pair of very elderly ladies who were talking to the desk worker about—to his surprise—one of the canaries. It slowly developed, through many stops and starts and much embarrassment, that the lady on the left had received one of the birds several weeks before, and she was expressing how much it had meant to her. Because of this, she had brought her friend down with her here to ask if she might have a bird too, but she wanted to be honest about it—her friend was blind. She knew she could care for the bird, and that it wouldn't be hurt, and she implied very gently how much just hearing it would mean to her friend, but she didn't want to get it under false pretenses.

The social worker was quite taken aback by the request and looked helplessly at Father for advice. Father quickly weighed the risk against the rewards and nodded his approval. Whereupon the lady who was talking whispered the situation to her blind friend who lit up with joy—and began very carefully to unfold a large, brown paper grocery bag she had brought along to bring the bird home in!

At this point Father stepped into the situation to see where he stood. It developed that the blind lady did have a cage at home, but it was very old and she was afraid to take it out on the bus, even though it would work very well if left on the dining table. She was sure that if they carried the bag very carefully, the bird would really be safer than if they took a chance on the very old cage. The situation, of course, was greatly complicated by the fact that the welfare department had no birds just to hand out, and there was nothing for the ladies to take home, even if they could. Father made a quick review of all the difficulties and the alternatives and concluded he'd better find out if the bird was really appropriate for the blind lady, and if it was, to get it to her at once.

He therefore took the couple with him to the car, drove out to our house without our realizing it, selected a bird, caged it, and took it off with his guests to the Santa Fe shop district. Here he had found a single room over a corner grocery store, immaculately clean—with one very antique birdcage sitting on a newspaper at the end of the dining table. The cage appeared to be sound, so, rather than insulting them by forcing the stout but seedy zoo cage on them, he transferred the bird over and rushed off, leaving them whispering to the canary.

The whole incident had a sharp effect on everyone involved in the zoo situation. Some way it was like reversing a pair of binoculars. We had all been so conscious of the waves of livestock pouring in, that they had sort of generalized to a blur. Then suddenly a single bird and its relationship to two people gave a reality to the whole operation.

Thus, by early fall, the bird situation seemed fairly well stabilized. The game birds were flowing into new pens at the birdhouse, and Father was thinning the small birds at a steady rate so that if everything held, he would have the back porch cleared by the first of November. This would satisfy his two strongest pressures: the need for getting everything into the garage which could be adequately heated come cold weather, and the imperative requirement of clearing the porch before Mother's fall meeting of The Art and Literature Club. The latter was of enormous importance.

It was essential that every evidence of "those birds of yours, Bernie" be gone before her friends arrived. Assisting hostesses would be bringing food and chairs and china in the back door. The driveway would be filled with cars. And no one must ever know about the livestock. Father could ignore a few "exceptions" and be grateful for the neighbors' discretion, but a faux pas in front of THE ART AND LITERATURE CLUB would threaten the foundations of the marriage.

And he probably would have made it had it not been for Tiglath-Pileser, the India hill myna.

# 6

# *Tiglath-Pileser*

Tiglath belonged to a wealthy family named Campbell who lived in Eastborough. Mr. Campbell was the owner of the Wichita Coca-Cola Bottling Plant and he was a member of the Rotary Club. One noon, shortly after Labor Day, Father had given an illustrated lecture to the Club on "Your City's Parks and Playgrounds" (no mention of the zoo beyond some fifty feet of film among the 1600 on the reel), but after the discussion, Mr. Campbell had caught Father on the way to the elevator.

"Fine talk, Bernie."

"Thanks, Mr. Campbell."

"Say, I saw in the paper about those animals you've been getting."

"Yes," Father replied somewhat wearily, "we certainly stirred something up."

"How'd you like an India hill myna?"

"I'm afraid I don't know what that is," Father said.

"It's a bird! You'd love it! I bought the thing in Mexico City for Evelyn, but we travel so much, we can't enjoy it as much as it deserves. Talks, you know! Be a great thing for the zoo."

"How do you mean, talks?"

"Oh, it says everything. Kind of a mimic. You don't have to teach it anything. It just copies what it hears. Whyn't you come and get it? You can have the cage, too, if you want it."

"Uh . . . Mr. Campbell . . . it sounds too valuable to risk it with the zoo's birds. We've got more than we can handle now, and Mr. MacDonald is a little touchy about our taking on anything we can't really care for. I'm just afraid . . ."

"How about your taking it yourself? Never mind the zoo. I'll give it to you personally. Your wife'd love it!"

He'd tripped a responsive chord in Father's mind. Father had been genuinely distressed at Mother's lack of affection for all the fascinating creatures he'd been bringing home, and the only explanation he could think of was that she didn't feel like they were really hers. If she had something she'd become attached to herself, he reasoned, she might be a bit more understanding about the birds in the garage. It was just possible that a little myna bird—which sounded unusually exotic—would do the trick.

"Well, all right. If you're really looking for a home for it—no strings attached—we'd love to have it."

"Great thing, Bernie. When can you pick him up?"

"Saturday morning be OK?"

"Fine. I expect to be there myself, but if I'm not I'll have the maid all ready with him. See you then."

So on the following Saturday morning, I was riding with Father on the way to get a bird for ourselves, for a change. The weather by now was cool and heading for that football-game-in-the-afternoon kind of smell, and it all looked promising.

We found the Campbell house and drove in off the street. Eastborough was Wichita's "exclusive" suburb where only the most select of the city's elite dwelt, and it was essential in Eastborough to have either the curving graveled drive, or the brick gateway with light globes on top. The Campbells were curved and driven.

Mr. Campbell was not there, but the maid was expecting us. We went down the hall to the huge kitchen in the rear, and there was the myna cage on the worktable in the center of the room. We were slightly taken aback by the size of the cage. It was a beautiful, stainless steel job about as long as a card table, and half as wide with height in proportion, and inside was this alert looking blackbird. The bird was about twice the size of a starling, but still smaller than a crow, ebony black, with a bright yellow beak and an orange face. It kept hopping about, cocking its head, and running its beak across the bars, but saying nothing.

We watched it a moment and thought it certainly looked

healthy and it sure was lively. Father asked what it ate.

"Fruit salad," he was told.

"Like what, specifically?"

"Well, you know, like a Waldorf salad? No mayonnaise, of course," the maid said, having her little joke. "You just pare an apple and chop it up, and then cut grapes in half, and dice up a banana, and that's it! If you can keep them in stock, he loves ant eggs sort of dusted on the fruit. After that, just some bird gravel on the floor and a little lettuce every few days and that's all he needs. He eats wonderfully, so you won't have any trouble."

"Doesn't he eat any seeds or bird feed?"

"No. Just fruit and ant eggs."

Father's enthusiasm was only slightly dimmed, so we put a newspaper over the top of the cage and took him out to the car, with the bird peeking out from underneath with the greatest curiosity.

The maid held the door for us, and as we went out she said, "Oh, yes. His name's Tiglath-Pileser."

"What!"

"Yes, Tiglath-Pileser. He's some sort of king in the Bible, Mr. Campbell says."

"How do you spell it?"

"I don't know. I've only heard it."

"Hmmm," said Father, and we passed on to the car.

The drive home was uneventful. Tiglath's cage sat on the back seat, and he jumped from one side to the other, stretching his neck to see over the window sills. We got him home and carried the cage between us into the kitchen and set it on the drainboard. Mother came out to see what we'd brought, and that look of instant affection which Father sought was singularly lacking.

"What on earth is that?" she asked.

"It's a talking bird from the mountains of India," said Father, trying to put its most appealing features first.

"What are you going to do with it?" came the second question, and this produced a long, somewhat obtuse discussion which did not actually say the bird was on its way to some place else, but at the same time never really said that it was going to stay with us either. Its diet had not been requested so was not volunteered. Thus it remained overnight. Then for one more day. Then through the rest of the week. Et cetera.

The first day, it never said a word nor uttered a sound. It was constantly in motion, however. It hopped from perch to side, to floor, to perch, to roof, to perch, to side, on and on. Since it weighed as much as a small chicken, each leap produced either a thud from perch or floor, or a ringing strum from the thin, steel bars. This tended to be somewhat fatiguing to us as the day wore on.

Sunday morning the bird was quiet and remained so until we lifted the dishtowel off after breakfast. Once in the light, it went bouncing from floor to perch to bars.

Shortly before church time, when the family was spread through the house preparing for departure, Tiglath leaned back and introduced us to the first of his two whistles. It cut its way down the halls and through the doors and caught all of us right across our temples. Whistle One was of the "Hey, there!" variety, and sounded like a Texan standing on a New York curb with his fingers between his teeth, signaling for a taxi about half a block away. While it never actually split glass, it did get attention. It was time for his breakfast.

Father hastily urged me to take Mother on to church, and he would stay behind to work up the fruit salad. Tiglath managed to get off several more blasts before I got Mother out the front door and brought the car around.

As we grew to know Tiglath, we found that he had a second whistle which was almost as penetrating, but which he used in a different way. It was more reflective, less demanding, and was something of a comment, rather than an order. It was the sort of throaty, "Hi, Sister!" expressed in the whistle of a regular Army sergeant watching three beauty parlor operators get off a bus about seven forty-five in the evening. Between the two salutes, Tiglath kept his presence felt.

Tiglath had a splendid appetite, even as we had been assured. When we came home from church, Father was washing the front of the kitchen cabinets, and the merest hint of a lunch showed on the edges of the cereal bowl in the cage. He had completed an apple, a banana, and several grapes as promised. There was the look of little labour, much health, about him.

The one flaw in this gourmand was his table manners. He would take a beakful of a banana, for example, and swallow what was inside his bill with relish, but this left him with the remains on both sides of his beak. Not wishing to drop the remains on his front, he would wipe his beak on the bars of the cage. This gave the effect of a giant-sized comb, which flipped food in all directions.

Regrettably, his schedule called for food at 10:00 each morning, and Sunday was the only day Father or I were home, so Mother got to know him better, and to know him was to loathe him, in her eyes. The preparation of the salad tended to be somewhat messy and could take up to ten or fifteen minutes, but the wreckage of the meal was so extensive that the cage had to be completely changed and the floor cleared for twenty minutes afterward. Mother immediately took to spreading out about four pages of the *Kansas City Star* on the kitchen floor, and then lugging the cage on to the middle of this field when she fed him, but the laying out and rolling up were nearly as bad as the original wiping down. The whole feeding operation, in fact, chilled that warm rapport that should have been the product of the care-and-dependence relationship.

The week progressed from day to day with Tiglath leaping about for hours on end and blasting out every so often —but without a word being said. I spent a good deal of the weekend and even more of the evening time I should have been dedicating to homework trying to elicit some dialogue. There was much "Hello!" and "Pretty boy!" and "Say good-bye, Tiglath" until an independent observer would have urged commitment, but there was not the tiniest hesitation in the perch, floor, perch, bars, perch pattern. On Thursday morning, however, during breakfast, Tiglath suddenly stopped hopping about, came to a full rest on a perch and said with expression, "Where are the keys, Chuck?"

We all three whirled around to look at him, and he hesitated for a moment, let go his taxi blast, and went back to hopping around. When we got home again that evening, Mother reported that she'd had nothing but hopping and whistling all day. Not another word. But during the evening, while we were all in the living room listening to the radio, there came from the half-darkened kitchen, "Over here, Charles, over here, Charles, over here, Charles, over here, Charles, over here, Charles . . . " We jumped up and sneaked toward the kitchen and he commented on and on. Finally we walked boldly in and turned on the light. He seemed neither to notice it nor us, and was sitting quite still on the perch saying, "Over here Charles, over here, Charles, over here, Charles . . ." like a moderate metronome.

These two incidents, we soon learned, were typical. The more familiar he became with his surroundings, the more he talked. Some days he seemed to be at it incessantly; other days he'd limit his remarks to a half dozen comments. We tried to show him off to company, and he was remarkably cooperative. Two-thirds of the time when a visitor would say, "Hello!" he would say "Elloelloelloelloello" back for a full minute. Most of the time, he would simply start talking to himself. There was no way of knowing what he would say, and he rarely repeated himself on successive days unless someone was greeting him in the same way.

As the previous owner had said, he was a mimic. He

never "learned" anything. As we got to know him, we found that what he said was stated in a very clear, feminine tone, which was quite opposed to the guttural croak of a parrot or parakeet. On the other hand, we found that what he said (which, incidentally, was almost always very easy to understand; no one ever asked, "What'd he say?") was usually expressed in vowels and plosives, and the listener was mentally supplying the rest of the word. The phrase, "Where are the keys, Chuck?" was really said, " 'air are the keeeees, Chuck?" but he would duplicate the inflexion of the question or phrase so perfectly that you were filling in the blanks yourself without realizing it. Some phrases like "Come in 'ere!" or "Cold tea" or "Turn it!" were reproduced precisely. Other words were pretty badly slurred. He could sound the Kansas City call letters KCMO as clearly as the announcer, but our local radio station, KFH, always came out "Kay-eff-ay." And while our "Chevrolet" was very blurred, "Chevvy" was always clean and true. He was delighted with t's, and a word like "tonight" was good for a hundred tries.

Indeed, it was the repetition that broke the spirit. At first we found this mimicry intriguing. We kept lists of the words he'd used, and we'd demonstrate him to anyone we could get to go into the kitchen. But one can only absorb a certain number of "tonights" until it loses the gay sparkle of novelty.

There was a hint of the water torture in it, too. Tiglath clearly got as much pleasure out of the rhythm of a word as he did out of the sound. Thus it was the rise and fall of a phrase like "back up and" pronounced "backupanbackupanbackupanbackupan" which made a sort of melody for him. The problem was that it made a sort of melody for the listener, too, so you assumed that it would follow a rational count and pattern. Thus if the bird hit a three-part beat on something, you instinctively expected him to say it eight times and stop. "Too hot," said as he said it, ought to be repeated seven times and abandoned. He would either do it six times or fifty. The result was you were either expecting another shoe to be dropped, or shoes were falling like hailstones. This was unbelievably wearing.

Between the hopping and feeding and the snappy dialogue, Mother cracked first, but soon even Father's cheer began to fade, and I was getting as distressed with his silences (when was he going to whistle next?) as I was with his repetition and noise. The result was an overwhelming vote: that bird had to go.

But go where? There was no place in the zoo picture to put it, and even though Father considered it ours, it seemed inappropriate to try to sell it locally when it had been received as a gift. This dilemma managed to waste a number of days, while we kept poor Tiglath in the basement with the light on. Mother maintained it was just as bad hearing him up the stair well as it was having him in the kitchen. By now it was too cold to put him outside, and worst of all, we were bearing inexorably toward the Night of The Art and Literature Club.

Driven by the imminence of this great date, Father finally decided he'd try the idea he'd been talking about for so long. A zoo trade. He therefore prepared a letter in which he said that he had an India hill myna which was inappropriate for his present display space, and he would be glad to trade it for any surplus cage birds that anyone had. Lovebirds or parakeets would be preferred, but a canary would be acceptable. Father refused to abandon his "a bird for Mother," and he thought he might be able to come out of the thing with something small and quiet. He sent copies of the letter to the zoos at Denver, Colorado Springs, Kansas City, Oklahoma City, San Antonio, and St. Louis. This was the middle of October.

One week, then two, went by. In the third, and thus into November and only ten days from "Art and Lit Day," he got a letter from San Antonio saying that if he still had the myna and wanted to part with him, they'd be happy to give him a home. Father came home waving the letter in triumph and he and I began furiously to build a shipping cage.

We ripped up empty cages in the garage, cannibalized a board from here and wire from there, and ultimately created a big wooden cage, five sides solid, with the face side covered with hardware cloth inside, and a fold-up, wooden cover on the outside. All this was so rigged that Tiglath's own cage was locked in the center, and a six-inch air space surrounded it on all sides. We worked out a complicated funnel and tube arrangement, so the express men could give him water from the outside, and wrote detailed instructions of "Live bird inside. Do not leave in unheated space." "Please pour one cup of water in this hole each morning and evening." "This side up," and various other graffiti appropriate to the occasion. We checked railroad schedules with care and selected times and routings that seemed the fastest with the least chance of chilling layovers. If all went well, it seemed we could put him on the Rock Island to Ft. Worth, where he could pick up the Santa Fe to Houston, and get the Southern Pacific on into San Antone. If he made every connection, he should be out the other end in a hair under two days.

Came the day of parting. We lugged him up from the basement with him shrieking his delight at every step. We gave his cage the final cleaning in the kitchen and as I scraped his perches he banged from one wall to the next saying "Paper porch, paper porch," at the top of his voice, having picked up a faulty version of Father's reply to the question, "Where's something for the bottom of the cage?"

We wired a coffee can to the floor of his cage, and loaded it with apples and ant eggs, thinking they would be the most likely to last out the trip. He was then locked into his wooden crate, and with the classic mixture of tears and relief, we plunged him into darkness for the last time. As a final gesture of camaraderie as we folded down the wooden access door, he sprayed three pieces of apple core and a seed across the front of our shirts.

He made the 4:30 for Fort Worth, and we returned from the express office exultant. Only eight days from the Art and Literature deadline and there was not a bird in the house nor a feather on the porch. Father had made it.

The actual week of the party Mother had us working like slaves. She checked off details and we were running out to borrow folding chairs at one place, extra dishes at another, nuts, mints, and sugar cubes from a third. All the rugs were cleaned and we had to walk on butcher-paper paths so as not to mess them up. The piano tuner spent half a day getting the baby grand in shape to carry the program, and Father was instructed which of our magazines were appropriate to the guests and could be shown face up in the rack, and which ones should be banished to the basement. By Saturday morning of the great event, Mother's list was down to about thirty final items that Father and I were responsible for, when the phone rang.

"This is Railway Express. You expecting some birds from San Antonio?"

"Yes, but we don't know when. Have you got a manifest on 'em? When are they due?"

"Due, hell. They're here now. I don't know where they've been, though. They're four days out of Texas, and from the looks of 'em, they ain't had food or water the while. You better get 'em out of here quick or all you'll need is a damage claim."

Father and I rushed out to the garage and took down a fairly respectable parakeet cage that someone had brought something in, filled up its water cups and poured some seed on the floor. With Mother yelling, "Where are you going? You don't have time to get mixed up in something now!" we ran out to the car and headed for the express office. We roared to a stop by the loading platform.

"My name's Goodrum. You've got a cage of birds for me, I hear. Where are they?"

"Right there," and he pointed to two of those big red and green baggage trucks they used to pull out beside the mail cars. On these trucks were stacks of egg crates and orange crates and lettuce crates and grapefruit crates, each lined with burlap and straw so you could neither see nor hear the contents, and each one was marked, "Live birds. Rush."

He handed us the invoice to sign, and it read:

| | |
|---|---|
| Parakeets, yellow | 100 |
| Parakeets, blue | 100 |
| Parakeets, albino | 6 |
| Finches, var. colors | 40 |
| Lovebirds, peach-faced | 10 |
| Lovebirds, Nyasaland | 10 |
| Cockatiel | 1 |

Father had not thought to find out what a myna was worth, and the San Antonio zoo, scrupulously fair, had made an honest trade.

Father stood there, looking at the inventory sheet and looking at the crates and looking at me. Minutes, literally, were a matter of life and death here. If these birds had been in shipment four days, it could well mean they were without food or water for five and cage birds begin to expire after three or four. It was November. There was no place at the zoo for them. We had destroyed most of the temporary cages that had been surplus in the garage. The back porch was unprotected and falling to 20 degrees every night. But they had to be gotten out of those shipping crates.

He shook his head and made a decision.

"Where's your phone?"

"In the office there."

Without having to look up the number, he dialed, and

then waited. The phone apparently rang and rang and rang.

Finally, he said, "Jim! I didn't know who was on today. Can you bring the pick-up truck to the Railway Express office absolutely at once? Bless you. I'll explain it when you get here. But drop everything and come right now. Okay? Thanks. See you."

"Come on, Chuck. Let's get as many of the smaller boxes into the car as we can. There's nothing to do but take 'em home."

I cringed at the enormity of what he was saying, but it was useless to comment. He knew as well as I did—indeed, clearly, much better—what this was going to cost him. The mind boggled.

Within fifteen minutes Jim arrived with the park truck and we began to load it. The Railway Express men were as worried about the insurance losses as we were about keeping the birds alive, and they pitched in feverishly. By putting crates both on the truck and in the cab, by shoving them all over our own sedan, we managed to get everything loaded for a single trip. Throughout all the activity there was not a sound or sign of life from the burlap walls. Both we and the express men feared the worst.

We dashed off for home, and along the way I got up nerve to ask, "Where are you going to put them?"

"There's nothing to do but just turn 'em loose in the basement. If we can figure out some way to keep them off the furnace, I think they'll be all right. As soon as we get home, you take a hammer and lift the hinge pins from the screen doors around the house. When you get the screens out, take 'em down and lean 'em around the outside of the furnace so the birds can't fly up against the hot walls. Then take off the window screens and cover the top. I don't think the ducts get hot enough to hurt them."

We got home and drove down the driveway, with Jim in the truck right behind us. Mother rushed out on the back porch and met us with, "Where have you been? What's all that?"

Father decided the only hope was a roaring offense, and by sheer force of activity and verbiage he began to get the crates past her, through the kitchen, and down the basement stairs. With him at one end and Jim at the other, they cleared the truck and the car, while I lifted door screens and then window screens and made a ramshackle-looking tepee around the furnace itself.

Mother watched the uproar, teetering between fury and despair. By the time I'd gotten all the bare, cast-iron portions of the equipment covered, Father and Jim had all the cages in, spread all over the place.

"All right, let's see what we've got."

We began to tear the slats off the crates, and then each of us reached the breathless moment of opening the burlap "sacks" that had been stitched into the crates with binding twine. I remember feeling a sort of sickening reluctance to flip back the cloth, not knowing whether I'd find a heap of dead birds or what. Throughout all our work the boxes had been as silent as slatted coffins. I gritted my teeth and ripped open the seam.

Inside, completely insulated from everything and living in a black world for five days, were twelve or fifteen parakeets. As I spread the burlap back, several looked up and tried to walk on the unsteady cloth. Two or three looked about and then flew up past my face and circled around the basement uncertainly, looking for a place to land. Two-thirds of the occupants were alive, but so weak that I could put my hand in and lift them on to the floor. I started an infirmary of the little things over beside the workbench where no one could step on them. All of the ones in my box were pale blue and so soft and light that they felt like the dried skins I'd used in biology class at school. One in my boxful was dead and had been trampled so that he was scarcely thicker than a piece of corrugated cardboard. The others crawled up the burlap with beaks and claws and teetered on the edges, apparently too weak to fly, but still lively enough to sit upright and move around.

Jim and Father were finding the same sort of thing in their boxes.

"Chuck, run out to the garage quickly and bring in food. We'll keep opening crates."

I climbed up the stairs, watching closely at each step for fear one of the birds had flown up and might be underfoot, and went out through the kitchen. In the garage, the bird-seed was kept in huge fifty-pound sacks, too big for me to carry, so I scooped up Mason jars that were stored along the wall and filled as many as I could hold full of the fine, polished seed. As I came back in, I met Father lifting all the cereal bowls and soup bowls out of Mother's cupboards and carrying them away in stacks. I beat on the door to frighten any birds which might have gotten to the top of the stairs, and the two of us went down, Father clumsily closing the door behind him without dropping his towers of china.

Once downstairs I began pouring seed on the floor in mounds around my "infirmary" and then along the walls, beside the water heater, and under the stairs. I was delighted to see the birds begin to eat almost as quickly as the feed hit the floor. Father was filling and setting water bowls around the room, and Jim was ripping open crates. Before long, the place was strewn with empty cartons, and there were birds everywhere. It became almost impossible to walk because of weak birds which had floundered out of the boxes or staggered away from where we'd set them down, and the air was getting thick with the ones who could fly, or were getting their strength back from the food. They were lining up on the overhead furnace ducts like sparrows on a telephone wire. They were sitting on top of window sills and the water pipes, and they were popping in and out of the little "X" supports on the floor joists. Eventually, every crate had been opened and we straightened up and looked around us. The whole room seemed to be in motion. The floor, the workbench, the stools, and the tables were seething, and the air was filled with birds going up or down or just flying around. We stood there and looked about, shaking our heads.

Father said, finally, "All right. There's nothing more to be done here for the moment. Let's get back up and help Mother. We can clear the crates away tomorrow. Right now, let's get the truck out of here, and see if we can get Mae calmed down. And be careful of the door. If any of these things got loose upstairs, it'd be the last straw." So we crept upstairs and left the feathery blizzard behind.

Jim drove off and the day ran out. Mother's lists were

checked off and accomplished. The fifty or sixty guests arrived dressed to the teeth, and the house filled overhead with Mother's Awful Secret hidden below. During the coming in, the female uproar drowned out anything in the basement, but as the house began to hush for the first soprano solo, the guests became aware of a strange sound which seemed to rise from the hot-air ducts. It had an all-pervasive note, issuing uniformly from all the rooms, and while not unpleasant, it was unusual and provoked a certain amount of behind-the-hand whispers. Mother refused to notice anything unusual, and the various guests who tried to project Do-you-hear-something, Mae? looks got only gracious smiles from Mother, who was apparently lost in the beauty of the music. Ultimately, the culture degenerated to refreshments, and the guestly chatter drowned out the cheeps for the remainder of the affair. Came midnight, the guests departed leaving the emptied house behind, filled with the soothing sound of some two hundred and fifty of her little feathered friends coming up through the floor.

The epilogue to the whole mess, which to this day my Mother blames on "that myna bird," went thus: almost all of the birds which were still alive when we got them recovered completely. There was possibly a ten percent loss in the whole shipment. Father selected pairs of the lovebirds, the one cockatiel, and all of the finches, and added them to the zoo's collection in the garage. The remaining hundred and seventy-five were put on the market. These birds, technically having no "municipal property" strings attached, were available for sale. Father's timing could not have been better. They came to us in mid-November, just before the

Christmas rush, and the local Grant's "dime store" agreed to pay approximately a hundred and fifty dollars for the lot, if we would hold them till the first of December. We were delighted to comply, and for two weeks I came home from school each evening, beat on the cellar door to clear the stairs, and then went down and fed the lot. I recall having read *Green Mansions* in school at about this time and thinking how wide is the gap between the novelist's world and life as it's really lived. If Rima, the bird girl, had dwelt so surrounded with her singing friends, she must have had the best-washed hair on the Amazon.

Later, after Father had begun building the zoo into a position where he was invited to zoological conventions, we learned that Tiglath-Pileser had arrived in San Antonio in half the time it took the other half of the deal, and that he was a tremendous success. While they had had mynas before, until that time none had even approached his sociability and keenness of ear. He became a favorite of the San Antonio papers who reported on what they described as "his increasing vocabulary," and many of the scientific assertions about mynas in the learned literature are based on observations of T-P.

All this was less important to Father than the one hundred and fifty dollars cold cash he had in his hand, which meant that for the first time in nearly a decade, the Wichita Municipal Zoo could *buy* an animal for the Lion House.

# 7

## *Incident of the Lion House*

And so, six months after the advent of the pelican, Father was at long last free to pursue the greater glorification of the zoo itself. When he'd heaved the bird over the fence for the first time, he thought he was on his way toward a great zoological garden. Instead, he'd shot half a year trying to sort his way out of that morass of pets and birds, all sandwiched in among his regular job of running baseball and tennis and golf tournaments, supervising swimming pools and outdoor theaters, and organizing twelve-hour-a-day programs in the parks themselves. He'd had no time for a really constructive thought on the zoo for weeks.

The long delay, however, had left him dealing from strength, for a change. The publicity on the odds and ends had doubled and redoubled the crowds, and the city was both aware of the zoo's existence and ripe for a little novelty and action. Most important, the Christmas sales of Tiglath's legacy left him with $150 hard cash, free and clear from any MacDonaldian strings. Came the first of the week past New Year's, and Father surveyed the status quo.

The large alligators were properly paralyzed and filed under the Lion House. The little caymans had refused to congeal, and so were transferred to the Bird House where they were scuttling over pans of water near the coal stoves in the flight cage. The finest bird specimens were wintering in the garage, warmed by two electric heaters that ate into our household budget without any hope of reimbursement (both too complicated and, under the circumstances, politically impractical). The small animals were thriving in the Bird House, and the bears were woolly and happy in the cold. Any outdoor expansion would have to wait for spring, so Father directed his attention inside—to the Lion House.

From the point of view of the visiting patron, the Lion House was in pretty fair shape. A chilled citizen coming in from a raw and windy afternoon found the place warm, clean, and flooded with light. The usual move of a visitor was to step through the doors and give a general, sweeping glance to the room with a "well, what have we here?" note, and then invariably end with his attention riveted to the second cage on the left. This was occupied by Simba, an absolutely superb Nubian lion. Simba would have been a credit to any zoo, and he was simply astonishing in ours.

Simba was at the full peak of his manhood at this time, and spent each day striding about the cage with his head up and his chest out, looking like something off a trademark. He had an unusually fine head and a full mane, and was manifestly aware of the figure he cut. Simba was an indoor lion and leaned heavily toward the inside half of his cage, but Saylor was convinced that "a little fresh air'll do you good," so through the sunny months he'd drive him out and drop the door behind him. This really fried him. With the clang still ringing in his ears, he would frown and stomp back and forth a few times and then come to a full stop with his front paws well apart—and cough. This cough was not unlike hitting an empty oil drum with a baseball bat, and the noise carried across Riverside Park into the neighboring residential districts with astonishing clarity. The odd thing was that the people who lived there never heard it, while people who visited them found it most unnerving. We were perpetually being told by the nearby neighbors, "You know, we never notice it ourselves, but my brother-in-law's family were here over the weekend, and they kept asking 'how do you stand it?' " Just before the 3:30 feeding, Simba would favor the crowds with some full-throated, rumbling roars, and shortly thereafter Saylor would let him inside to eat and bed down for the evening. With this, Simba would take on the satisfied look of a day well spent.

Thanks to his natural indoor tendencies, he enjoyed winter best of all. What with never having to go out, he could hold the full attention of the crowds all day, and the combination of the steam heat under the armpits and the cool, concrete floor when you stretched out, seemed to provide the sublime condition for the good life. From Thanksgiving to Easter he strode about with slow dignity. By afternoons he rarely moved at all, spending most of his time standing at a three-quarter slant, looking imperious.

Simba was a great believer in the well-ordered life. He liked things in proper sequence and operating according to schedule, and in this he agreed with Jim Poindexter's approach to zoomanship. Jim would come in at 7:30 in the morning and get the lights on and the public floor swept while Saylor was carving meat in the kitchen. After sowing the mosaic with cedar sawdust and sweeping everything neatly from one end to the other, Jim would go over to the cat cages and get them scrubbed clean before the public arrived.

The routine started with Simba and was worked like a Chinese block puzzle. There were five large cages on the side. The center cage was left empty until cleaning started, at which time Jim would unlock the levers and raise the door between Simba and the empty cage. Jim would start chanting, "Aw ri', let's go, let's go!" and Simba would give him his "I was intending to anyway, so why not?" look and very casually stroll from his cage into the empty center one. Jim would then let the bars drop with a crash.

He would next unlock the levers to the left and open the door between Simba's cage and King, the young male in the first cage. King would dutifully slip into Simba's cage and Jim would let that door drop. He would then unlock the big door facing out into the center of the room, shove a hose inside, and get the water running. With everything sloshing away, he'd grab a broom and jump up inside the cage himself. He'd flood the place and scrub it down then jump out and lock the door behind him. As soon as most of the water was drained away, he'd let King back in, and do the same job on Simba's cage.

Shortly before Christmas, Father had inadvertently jarred this careful sequence and the results were dramatic. Father tried to hush up the whole affair, and we'd probably never have heard about it at all, if the Chief Forester hadn't asked him a direct question in front of me. Father made him swear it would never get back to Mr. MacDonald and then sketched out the following.

It seemed that he had been on the way to North High School for an early meeting and on an impulse had stopped by Riverside and come up to the Lion House well before it opened. The "Closed" curtain was down, but he could hear Jim's hose spraying inside so he'd rapped on the glass and yelled to Jim to let him in. Jim eventually heard him, and leaving the hose lashing around on the floor, had jumped out with the broom in hand to unlock the door. Father greeted him warmly and the two got involved in a discussion in the middle of the room. Several minutes along, Father happened to look over Jim's shoulder and to his horror saw Simba leaning out through the open cage door, surveying the scene. Before Father could react, Simba crouched and sprang completely across the aisle behind the guardrail and landed with a quiet thud out in the main public area of the room.

In Father's words, "I nearly had a heart attack! There was that lion loose in the room, starting to walk up behind Jim and Jim just talking to me as casual as hell not even knowing it was out.

"I tried to freeze perfectly still, and without raising my voice, I said, 'Jim, don't move. There's a lion out behind you. He's loose and coming toward you. What'll we do?'

"Instead of holding still like a sane man, Jim just turned around in that deliberate way of his and said, 'Simba, what you-all doing there? You get back in that cage. Do you hear me?'

"The lion stopped and just stood there about one good leap away. I put my hand behind me very slowly to see if I could find the door handle, and I couldn't even find the door, much less the knob. Jim just went on talking. He was sort of rambling like, 'You get back in that cage. You get back, you hear me! What you doin' out for Heaven's sake? You know you don't belong out here. You get back in, I tell you,' and stuff like that."

Father said, "You never see a lion right next to a man, and you don't realize how big the things are. Simba weighs almost four hundred pounds, and he stands so tall he was looking up at Jim and it seemed like all he'd have to do was breathe and poor Jim'd be knocked flat. I was so worried about Jim, I forgot to think how I was going to get out myself. Jim had this broom in his hand—just an ordinary kitchen broom, not the push kind—and he just raised it up with the bristles pointing in front of him and aimed them at the lion's eyes. All the time he was easing forward very slowly and the broom kept getting closer to the lion's face and all the time he kept on talking.

"Just as the broom got so another step would drive it into its eyes, the lion sort of twisted his head to the side and stepped back. Jim kept coming and talking and Simba backed off another step to keep the broom out of his face. The lion kept backing and Jim kept talking till he got the animal completely across the room and up against the guardrail in front of the leopards' cage. For the first time, I noticed that every animal in the room was standing stock still watching Jim and the lion.

"When the lion backed up against the railing, he slid back along it for a step or two and then reared back and jumped forward—up over the rail and down in the little aisle between the guardrail and the wall under the cage fronts. When he jumped, I thought he was coming at Jim and I nearly fainted.

"Jim kept right on coming with the broom until he got up to where the lion was crouched down looking sort of puzzled. You could see he couldn't account for the wall behind him, and he hadn't realized the cages were over his head.

"With the lion cramped back in the aisle, it seemed to me that Jim could run to the door behind me and we could get outside before the animal could get to us. Once we got outside, I thought I could hold the door while Jim got around to the back to warn Saylor, and then we could get some nets and a gang of men and come back in strength—with a good rifle in case anything got out of hand. I was about to whisper to Jim to make a dash for it, when he lifted up the broom and slammed it down on the lion's rump with a thud. When he hit him, he said, 'Now you get up in there, do you hear me? You get up. Get up. Get back in that cage. You get! Hurry up!'

"All the time he was swatting away and yelling at the

lion and I thought any minute the lion was going to charge him for sure. Instead, you could see the lion was completely confused. Here he was being beaten on, he was squeezed down there in a strange place, people were shouting at him, and all he wanted to do was go home! Sure enough, he finally figured it out, and he jumped up through the open cage door. Jim just walked up and leaned over the rail and slammed it shut, and then he rolled over the railing and snapped the lock through and closed it. And it was all over."

Father reported, "I tottered over and leaned on the rail beside him and I told him, 'Jim, don't you ever take a chance like that again.' I told him that lion could have jumped him at any moment, and I gave him flat instructions that if anything like that ever happens again, he's to get out. I told him, 'We can get enough people together so that nobody'll get hurt, but don't you ever try that one-man business again, do you understand?'

"Jim just looked at me with a sort of tolerant grin and said, 'Bernie, I don't need nobody else. He wasn't going to do nothin'. He was just as scared as you was. Scareder. He hadn't never been out of that cage in his whole life. He didn't know where he was at or what to do next. You just got to tell him. He ain't mad at nobody.'

"I said, 'Do you think he knew you were his friend?'

"Jim says, 'Naw. He don't know who I am. He's just a dumb animal. He don't know me from Adam.' "

Father, who was a full-time romantic, refused to accept this. He was convinced that Jim was just covering a deep feeling of mutual affection, and that Jim and that lion understood each other as only the closest of friends can.

Father went out and got Saylor and the three of them collected around the cage to review the situation. They finally agreed on what had happened. Jim had moved Simba and dropped the door, and moved young King and closed him in. He'd cleaned King's cage and moved him back and was working in Simba's cage when Father beat on the door. Jim had jumped out and while he was away, Simba apparently had been nosing around the connecting door to his temporary space and had discovered that the sliding bars had gotten crosswise on their rails and had failed to drop clear to the cage floor. This was most unusual, since the panel weighed seventy-five or eighty pounds and the only way it could even be raised was with the lever and pulley arrangement on the outside.

This time, however, it had apparently stuck a few inches above the floor, and Simba, probably through curiosity, had gotten his nose under it and then lifted it high enough so that he could scramble back into his own cage. Once there, he'd apparently been puzzled to find he could look right out into the room through the open cage door. Nothing ventured, nothing g., he must have thought he'd have a go at it, and had simply jumped out to see what lay on the other side of the mountain.

The question of what he might have done if either he or the men had panicked always sort of hung in the air. There was no doubt that the leopards were eager to claw someone, and as we'll see a new keeper was badly mauled by a bear the following year, but whether Simba's higher intelligence and rather calm spirit actually made him as tame and rational as he appeared was something we never resolved for sure.

The name "Simba," incidentally, reflected a strange phenomenon that was loose on the prairies in the Thirties. No one thought of painting "Simba (Swahili for lion)" on the cage. The fact was that nine-tenths of the visitors to the zoo knew perfectly well what "simba" meant, and indeed considered themselves something of an expert on lions in general and African lions in particular.

This weird bit came about because those were days of the freewheeling adventure writer. Richard Halliburton, Frank Buck, Raymond Ditmars, and others were off to the far distant lands and came back loaded with books and pictures. Kansas had its own explorers and we followed them inch by inch across Africa and through the jungles of Southeast Asia. Their names were Martin and Osa Johnson and in their day not only did their zebra-skin bindings appear on all the coffee tables of Kansas, but they made the Book-of-the-Month regularly and their movies made a mint on the Fox and Keith circuits.

Before coming to Wichita, we'd lived in a middle-sized, southeastern Kansas town called Chanute, and this was right in the heart of Johnson country. The result was I was even more deeply dipped in the lore than most. Martin Johnson had been a clerk in a photographic store in nearby Independence where he'd been seized with a classic case of the wanderlust. Rather than thinking about it, he'd done something, and through an unlikely series of steps got himself a job as cook with Jack London when London sailed for the South Seas aboard *The Snark*. They all explored the head-hunting country of Borneo and New Guinea together, and when they got home, Johnson took to giving illustrated lectures of his travels in the local theater.

Having a real-live explorer only fifty miles away was enough to flush out the cultural leaders of Chanute and they made the pilgrimage south on the Santa Fe. The show was a little strong on hand-tinted stereopticon slides, but it took our friends and neighbors off to the far-distant and they thought the trip (both theirs and London's) a great success. For some reason that is no longer quite clear, the prettiest girl in Chanute's high school had been asked to come along to sing Hawaiian songs during intermission. In any event, this had a molten effect on Martin who promptly fell in love with her—Miss Osa Leighty—and for the next two decades they ground around the unexplored world together.

Osa was a cute, sort of plump, little lady with bright eyes, who soon developed into one of the deadliest game shots in Africa. Martin would man the movie cameras, and Osa would drop charging rhinos at the foot of the tripod. We lapped it up.

They'd be off on the veldt for a year or so, and then suddenly would fly into the Chanute airport in their two amphibian planes, and all of us kids would bicycle out and spend hours looking at the black and white one painted like a zebra and the tan one painted like a giraffe. When I was in grade school I lived in the same block with the Brinkerhoff girl whose dad flew one of the planes. This was real living. And as if that weren't exciting enough, Martin used to go to the local Rotary Club meetings while they were home, and Father always led the singing before the canned fruit and after the chicken a-la-king. On one occasion, he had remarked how difficult it was to get lantern slide glass any more, and Martin had said, "Let me give you some old stuff I have. You can boil the gelatin off and they'll come clear for whatever you need them for."

Father thereupon brought home about two hundred slides *actually taken on the cruise of The Snark!* I carefully held them up to the bridge lamp and was somewhat startled to find they were all hand-tinted pictures of natives with advanced stages of elephantiasis. Johnson had put this collection together for talks to medical societies, I guessed, but the audience couldn't have been too broad, and no wonder he was willing to have them boiled away. I found them very educational, revealing various things I didn't know even existed, much less in these shapes. When Father found time to examine them they disappeared and I have no idea where they are today. I know he thought "real Johnson pictures from the *Snark* voyage" were too good to destroy —but their use was even more limited in our household than in Johnson's.

The slides were fine, but, like the rest of the Kansans, for us the books were the real things. I spent hours trudging by their side on safari. *Congorilla. Four Years in Paradise. I Married Adventure.* They were both masters of the italic form of travel writing. You'd go sailing along with a smooth bit of prose and all of a sudden fall over those genuine dialects of the Dark Continent: "I had M'pishi bring me the saddle and the *biltong* he carried with him." "There beside the ivory hunter's *boma* at the edge of the *donga* was a hartebeest thrown against the mud wall." "And so as the sun set, we emptied the guns and gave our *kikuyu* a generous *bakshishi* before we returned to camp." I rarely had the faintest idea what the italics meant, but, by George, they were authentic and gave it just that note of truth that kept me plowing page after page.

There were some words I did understand, and "simba" was one of them. I don't think Martin or Osa Johnson ever mentioned a lion in their lives, but we had "simbas" we hadn't even talked about yet. "Simba" was the real thing.

Us kids in Chanute had maps we followed the Johnsons on (Osa would write her mother, and Mrs. Leighty would tell the *Tribune*), and possibly my first great shock was reading that the Johnsons had been involved in an airplane accident in—the incredibility of it—Los Angeles, California. A scheduled airline coming in from Salt Lake City had crashed with them aboard, and Osa was badly hurt and Martin was killed. Martin was brought home to Chanute, and the funeral was held in the Chanute Memorial Hall over the fire station. Three thousand people filled the seats and lined the corridors and steps outside. I remember they used the painted backdrop of a forest we had for high school graduation ceremonies, and they set the huge casket on an artificial grass mound in the center of the stage. When everything was quiet, they began playing sound tracks from his wildlife pictures, and for almost an hour we listened to the sounds of the islands and the jungles and the veldt, and at the end they closed the curtains and he was buried in the Chanute cemetery. I must have been about twelve at the time, and I was deeply affected by the whole experience.

I've long suspected this familiarity with the Johnsons' life among the wild animals may have been the base for Father's attachment to the zoo, and subtly permitted him to assume more of a knowledge of the beasts than he even approached. In the Thirties, there was very little literature available on the actual running of a zoo, and except at the great zoological gardens at London and The Bronx and the like, most zoomanship was handed down from keeper to keeper by word of mouth. The result was, that from many conversations, Father soon knew as much about the mechanics of our operation as either Jim or Saylor.

Our lions, for example, were fed six days a week on horsemeat. At regular intervals, Saylor would drive the zoo truck up north of town to the dessicating plant, and buy one dead, but refrigerated, horse carcass. He would back the truck up to the zoo kitchen door and he and Jim would struggle the horse into the walk-in refrigerator and then he would carve away on it through the week. Simba got ten pounds of meat chunks Monday, Wednesday, and Friday, and young King got eight. They got no bones to avoid the chance of slivers catching in the intestinal tract, so on Tuesdays and Thursdays their servings were scored and bone meal and cod liver oil was packed down in the cuts. On Saturday they got ten pounds or so of the raw liver and kidneys, and on Sunday they fasted. This day without food gave rise to some pretty spectacular roaring for the customers, but it was traditional and nobody dared challenge it. Much, much later, we learned it was actually based on logic. Since a lion in the wild cannot—or at least does not—kill every day, their systems actually require regular periods of fasting, and if they were to be fed every day, it would drastically shorten their life span.

A lion has a remarkably clumsy way of eating, incidentally. The huge fangs which are so apparent are really designed for seizing the food in the chase and holding it. They don't meet properly and they keep the front incisors from shearing, so a lion has to tear and chew with his side teeth. This causes him to eat on the bias and gives him the look of being suspicious of his fellow diners. The fact is, he can't help it.

Simba, like all lions, gave this impression of watching out of the corners of his eyes, but in truth not only did he have no one threatening him from the cleaning cage on his left, young King on the other side was both his son and a great friend of the Old Man's. They got along very well, and probably could have been put into the same cage if there had been any need for it. (This wasn't even considered, of course. With such a limited supply of animals, half the idea was to stretch the population as far as it could go. In the summer months, Saylor always left the door of the empty cleaning cage open to the outside range in hope that people would think that "whatever was in there" must be outside. By the time they'd go outside, it apparently had gone back in.)

Young King was the product of Simba and Mary some four years back, and had now reached young manhood. He was much lighter than his father and would never have the mane the old man did, but he had a fine head and profile and would make good breeding stock now that he was old enough to mate. Mary, his mother, had passed to her reward the year of the great blizzards, a victim of advanced age and probably of the heating difficulties of the winter, although she hadn't died until late spring, just failing to wake up one morning.

The aging of lions, by the way, is a difficult thing for zoos. It takes a lion about three years to reach sexual adulthood, and then they look splendid for display until they're about ten years old. From ten to fifteen they lose their apparent vigor and begin to lack the "snap" of good exhibition material. Then from fifteen to twenty, even though they are in perfectly fine health, they seem to be so sickly and decayed that the visiting public is distressed just looking at them. Their hair falls out in patches, their lips fail to close properly, and they develop an unfortunate sway in the back. The result is that they are an embarrassment to the zookeeper. He's usually grown fond of the animal, and he knows it's still healthy and happy in his declining years, but the criticism he draws from the visiting public makes him liable to the ASPCA. The result is that when one like Mary goes to sleep at fifteen, the keeper feels more relief than sorrow.

King was now four and Simba only eight, so we would have no geriatric problems for some time to come. We did need a female, though, and this would have to be an early order of business.

The fourth cage, the unit beyond the cleaning cage, held two jet black leopards. They were both males and they were just as cruel and malevolent as they looked. They would literally lie against the front bars and when anyone came anywhere close a black paw would slash out in hopes of snagging something. All large cats have to have some means of cleaning their claws, and because of this each of the cages had a peeled log in it. The two lions would scrape their paws down theirs in a casual way after eating, but the leopards spent hours ripping their log down the length of the grain. They gave every evidence of biding their time, confident that their chance would come. Someway a reverse myth has built up nowadays that only tigers are really man-killers in the wild. This is patently untrue. A recent government report from India records over three hundred persons killed by what appeared to be a single leopard in the short span of three years. The Superintendent of the Uganda Protectorate reported 17 natives killed by lions in his area between 1955 and June of 1956. Between television nature studies and the ease with which trained animals are handled at the circus, we forget that even a hundred-pound leopard can be extremely dangerous. While waiting their chance, our leopards ate the same rations as the lions (though cut to three-pound servings each) and kept their strength up. Unlike the lions, leopards live to twenty years without any apparent decay at all!

The final cage on the left side held two very gentle cheetahs. Whether it was by contrast to the clear-cut personalities of Simba and the leopards, or whether they just were pretty colorless, they seemed to be short any real distinction. They were lithe and slim and spent most of their time lying down but looking alertly out toward the crowds. Cheetahs can be tamed to walk on a leash and are used extensively in India as hunting animals, somewhat like the medieval use of falcons for killing and returning game. I don't think anyone ever gave any real thought to working with ours, and so they spent their time consuming their horsemeat and an occasional pigeon. They looked alert, but not too bright.

The other side of the Lion House was made of seven narrower cages which held a mess of odds and ends—all some kind of a monkey. These were thrown together or sorted apart without regard to zoological classification, but simply by who got along with whom. The result was an illogical sort of mixture, but it seemed to work out, and every cage had someone leaping about or swinging around—which after all is all you can ask of a monkey display.

If there was any zoological theme to our primate collection, it came through the fact that the monkeys we had were the hardiest varieties available, and the longest lived. About half of them were little brown rhesus, which are almost indestructible. The monkey cages, like the larger cat cages, had outside runs as well as indoor display areas, and the rhesus probably could have survived either in or out. They live for fifteen or twenty years, and ours were all ages and sizes.

We had a pair of capuchins with their little skullcaps and their looping tails carried over their backs, and a very active pair of spider monkeys which were kept in the largest of the right side cages. With their short bodies and long arms and legs, they swept back and forth from swing to bars to floor, with someone always in motion. The tiny little squirrel monkey I had welcomed in the summer had increased in size and joined a cageful so he was thoroughly accepted. He seemed to recognize me and would take peanuts from my fingers, but he no longer needed human companionship and, while cordial, could take me or leave me alone. Regardless of variety, the monkeys all ate the same things—which pretty much amounted to what the nearby grocers had left over on their vegetable counters at the end of the day. Anything that was bruised, bent, or wilted, was left in crates beside the back door, and Bob Saylor would pick them up in his own car on the way to work. He would analyze this residue in the kitchen, cutting off tops and dissecting black spots, and then what was salvageable was slid into the monkey cages. This ran heavily to carrots, celery, lettuce, cabbage, and sweet potatoes. On good days, it would have an occasional banana in it or some apples, and during each feeding Saylor would flip in one piece of bread per monkey, which he bought from the nearest bakery as "day-old and reduced."

The peanut ration rose and fell with the size of the viewing crowds, but in total was fairly substantial. It provided an important source of needed protein and warmed Mr. MacDonald's heart. Everyone was happy: the visitor's initial purchase gave a profit to the concessionaire, the peanuts filled a gap in the diet, Mr. MacDonald saved the cost of buying food, the monkeys enjoyed them, and the children got lots of healthy, satisfying exercise firing the shells through the bars. Between the vegetable bar and the peanut offering, the monkeys thrived.

Father walked round and round the Lion House, staring at the animals and mentally shifting the occupants from one cage to another. Someday—as soon as possible—he had to get a mate for young King. For the moment, he didn't know just how.

He did have $150 in hand and the situation appeared to call for something small enough to fit in an emptied monkey cage, big enough to be seen, cheap enough to fit the budget, and sufficiently long-lived to get some return on Tiglath's money. It had to be something that thrived on either horse-meat or leftover supermarket vegetables, and could withstand a possible drop in the temperature. Finally, it had to be strange enough looking that the crowds would know it was new and different when they went by.

Father wrote off to Trefflich's in New York for a catalogue. Back it came, listing rare and exotic animals like a seed catalogue shows roses. Father brought it home and spent evenings eliminating this and adding up points for that. The only real trouble was that Trefflich Bird and Animal Company assumed that most of its clients had some idea about what it was selling. It therefore felt little call for the descriptive passages and instead got right down to the heart of the matter:

| | | |
|---|---|---|
| Zebra, male | 2-year old | $1500 each |
| Camel, pair | 2-year old | $4000 pair |
| Otters, male or female | mature | $125 each |
| Tortoise, Galapagos | 200 lb. | $800 each |

and so on. Father would make notes of those within his price range, and then go down to the Public Library during the evening to see what the thing was and what it ate. The Library had nothing that even approached a manual of zoological practice, but a combination of two veterinary textbooks and the Encyclopaedia Brittannica worked surprisingly well. Through much note taking, many books consulted, and hours of wishful thinking, his list began to look like

Bobcat—small, eats horsemeat, lives 10 years. Does best in outdoor cages
Pacas—only live three years
Lemurs—look too much like monkeys—already have plenty of monkeys
Peccaries—look too much like pigs
Anteaters—exotic looking, fairly hardy, food OK, only live five years, $125 each
Armadillos—sleep all day, move at night. Keep trying to dig through concrete floors
Sloths—sleep 18 hours out of 24. Cost $75

Finally he was down to one entry:

Coatimondi—big enough to see (four feet long) eat fruit, raw vegetables, and ground horsemeat; exotic appearing, rear legs twice as long as front legs, reasonably hardy, very friendly, active in morning and evening, quiet, clean, belongs to raccoon family. Cost $100 and express

"Mae!" Father announced triumphantly, "I'm going to buy a coatimondi."

"That'll be nice," said Mother. "What is it?"

"It's a big brown thing with a long thin snout and a long

bushy tail that looks like an anteater. It's related to the pandas, the book says. Doesn't look anything like 'em, but that'll look good on the sign."

"Does it eat ants?"

"No, no! Eats the same sort of things the monkeys eat. No trouble at all."

"How do you get them?"

"So far as I can see, all you do is fill out this coupon in the back of the catalog and they'll send one to you."

"Where are you going to keep it?" She sounded casual, but I realized this was the question we'd been headed for from the start.

"We'll put some more of the monkeys together and open up one of the small cages in the Lion House. I'll have 'em do it as soon as I order the thing, so we'll be ready for it no matter when it arrives."

"That's good, Bernie. I hope you'll be happy with it."

Father filled out the catalog coupons, counted the circles on the map to find which express zone we were in when Trefflich's was the center of the world, added this to the total cost, and mailed it all in an air-mail envelope.

As excited as we all were, we were still astonished to get the call from the express office less than five days later, "You've got some kind of an animal down here."

Father rushed over from City Hall, Saylor rolled the park truck down from the zoo, and I caught a bus from high school. We converged at Railway Express and there it was, a splendid crate looking like it had come straight from the Amazon jungles, big enough to hold a refrigerator. The boards were too close together for us to see anything, but the water pail was full and there was movement inside. We rushed it out to the zoo, laid boards from the open cage door across the guardrail and, with the help of a bunch of WPA workers who were building wire corrals under the trees, struggled the crate up onto the boards. Father dramatically knocked out the cleats holding the sliding door, lifted it, and out staggered one coatimondi. It wasn't quite as large as the crate suggested, but it was still big enough to attract attention, and it was exotic-looking like crazy. It had worked just like ordering from Sears and Roebuck. Father was delighted.

The reporters came, features were run, no new discards appeared, we were on the way at last.

# 8

# *The Joad Family Returns*

Father's penury and his plans for trading his way out of it were scarcely unique. All zoos are fiscally marginal. Since they must be funded out of the public till, and since there's never enough to go around, their dollars have to be held up against the repairs to the orphanage, another police car, beds in the municipal hospital, books for the school library —almost anything you think of can be more easily justified than spending tax money on a glorified pet store. By the same token, when the political leverage hits City Hall, the amount of pressure you can build up for a new gnu can be put in a gnat's eye. This has always been so, and one is hard pressed to say it isn't as it should be.

Notwithstanding this pitiful position, zoos have thrived in various sizes and shapes since the Caesars and at least half of the explanation hangs on inherent production. Logical progression: zoos show animals. Since animals come in two models, zoos show pairs of animals. Pairs of animals produce small-sized duplicates. (Digression: people would rather look at the small-sized duplicates than at the parents.) Small types grow up. Grownups take up space. Space runs out quickly. Query: what do you do with the surplus stock? Why, you trade it to other zoos, of course, who haven't got enough money to buy what you don't want.

The result is a constant ebb and flow of material. The difficulty comes with zoos that want something and have nothing to trade, and zoos that have lots of something that nobody wants.

One of the strangest aspects of this barter business is the way certain zoos seem to produce certain things without really intending to. Animals which have never bred anywhere in captivity will suddenly start reproducing in one collection and for years they will go through generation after generation. The National Zoo in Washington, for example, has been spraying pygmy hippopotami like a fountain for decades. Few zoos seem able to raise orang-utans like the Philadelphians. The Dublin zoo, of all places, and the park in Leipzig were the primary source of half the lions in cages back in the old days. Dublin had produced over four hundred lion cubs up through the Thirties, and Leipzig exported over seven hundred lions in just thirty-five years before World War I.

The great collections tend to trade among themselves since they deal in pretty esoteric varieties, but the small, municipal zoos develop specialties, too. In our part of the country, you always got lions from Oklahoma City, and *mirabile dictu*, even Wichita had its claim to fame. We begat small black bears like guinea pigs. The demand for small black bears wasn't everything that it should be, but if you could use one, Wichita could be counted on to have a surplus. This was to be Father's entré to the market.

Father had finally got a picture of the zoo he was headed for, drawn in his mind's eye. Like all good projects of the bureaucracy, it was to be built in stages. The first order of business was to get a mate for King. This should pick up an adequate amount of publicity, and get the Lion House in reasonably good shape.

Come spring, things could get started outdoors. Here his plan was to stretch out space with bulk, to create the illusion of a substantial collection. The idea was first to build cheap wire pens on the outerside of the curving zoo paths and fill them with deer, bison, and elk—which he hoped to trade for "locally"—and then begin to buy into antelope, zebras, llamas, and camels, if he could get donations going. In the meantime the only outlay would be wire and fence posts, and he suspected they cut enough hay off the airport and the parkways to give him most of the feed he'd need.

The small game animals he'd acquired during the discarded pet confusion could be housed in slightly more elaborate outdoor pens (they needed top wire and weather-tight houses), but judiciously spaced could use up considerable ground. He already had his fox, the badgers, the possums, raccoons, coyotes, and the ground hog. The porcupine had expired during the winter—to everyone's astonishment. It was supposed to have come from Canada, so the cold shouldn't have hurt it, and it had been eating corn and raw vegetables as happily as could be. It weighed over thirty pounds when it passed on, so it hadn't starved to death. Father researched the porcupine situation after its demise and found that they rarely live beyond four or five years, so the odds were that ours had put in most of its time before it joined us. He figured he could beg a wolf off the Fish and Game Department, and by a little duplication, could create a two-hundred-foot row out of the ten or twelve pens of the "American game section."

Another section of the walkways could similarly be filled with game birds. These, too, took slightly more elaborate, covered pens, but they still were mostly cheap wire with only a minimum of lumber involved, and once covered with park green would take up even more space than the animals. Thanks to their long tails, you expected a pheasant to have at least a seven by nine piece of ground—and all pheasants required for food was a little chicken feed thrown on the ground with some discarded lettuce occasionally. He had ringnecks, a pair of mutants, and some goldens on hand. It shouldn't be hard to find some silvers, some Lady Amhersts, and some Reeves. Add to these a pen of the Chukar partridges and the prairie chickens he had in the garage, and you'd filled up another hundred feet with a minimum of outlay.

Father had his own philosophy of small zoo display technique. He was convinced that if you couldn't provide something elaborate to house the exhibit in, you should paint the whole thing as unobtrusively as possible, see that the specimens looked healthy, and then PAINT A BIG

SIGN. The more information you got on the sign, the greater enjoyment the visitor got, he would explain.

"Have you noticed when a mother takes the kids to the zoo, she always stands there and reads every word out loud? The kids don't give a darn, but mother's sure it's good for them. And you've seen the compulsive readers, haven't you? It's usually the wife. She will recite every last syllable to the old man, as if he's illiterate and blind. Actually, I'm all for it. It increases everyone's enjoyment of the exhibits—free guide service . . . adds audio to the visual!"

Father was consistent with his moral. His signs covered a quarter of the cage front on occasion, but by the time you'd worked your way to the bottom, you'd gotten the feel of the specimen. You knew the English name, the Latin name, seen a map of its normal range, read about its native habitat, noted its nearest kin, explored its preferred diet, probable longevity, and Christian name. Father conferred a name on every live thing in that zoo on the conviction that people felt closer to the display if they thought it was someone special. This used to drive poor Jim and Bob Saylor crazy.

"D'ya get Renfrew moved?" Father would ask.

"Who?"

"Renfrew! The timber wolf. You know!"

"Oh. The wolf. Yeah, it's OK," and Saylor would give Jim just a hint of a long-suffering wince.

We had quite a collection of owls left over from the pet stock, and Father had a good place for several owl sheds, with a potential spot for some hawks which were not immediately in hand, but shouldn't be hard to pick up. These could be fed any of the rats Peterson might bag, and when that supply was missing, they could eat horsemeat scraps.

All of these displays were within immediate sight. He either had or could easily get the exhibits, and the WPA labor could put the pens together with a minimum of effort. Once these were up—and the cumulative number would provide many hundred feet of pens—it should make the central walks fairly full. He hoped the next step would sell itself. In various corners of Riverside, he built imaginary Children's Zoos with storybook animals. He paced out a monkey island. He erected mental goat mountains (complete with dyed concrete). A seal pool. Then (though they were still fairly cloudlike even in Father's imagination), splendid moated exhibits of elephants, giraffes, rhinoceroses, all in native habitat groups—and all donated in some yet undescribed manner. And, of course, a graceful new bird house, a perfect jewel of design, the first new building in twenty-five years, and the object of visitors from all over the country.

At this point in the fantasy the firm figure of Alfred MacDonald would rise in Father's thoughts and it was hard to see around him. MacDonald watched the zoo activity with a mixture of surprise, distrust, and awe. He was genuinely astonished that the pet confusion had sorted itself out with no more distress than it had. He was amazed and quietly pleased at all the newspaper copy the zoo kept receiving, and certainly the use of all the parks was rising steadily. The Park Department budget was done on a fiscal year rather than a calendar year, and though there seemed to be more animals running around one place and another, the feed-grain bill had risen only slightly and there seemed little change in the horse consumption. He suspected that Father would be asking for more money for the next year, but he hadn't said anything yet, and he would face that when Father brought it up.

MacDonald's use of Depression labor was unique in the Wichita scene. Wichita had been hit by the Crash and subsequent collapse as badly as any community. The three airplane factories had closed. The milling business laid off men as the dust killed the wheat crops. Two of the four packing houses closed down and Cudahy and Dold were working on fractional shifts. The Santa Fe had closed its roundhouses and repair shops, and the collapse of all these major payrolls had thrown thousands of families out of work and wrecked the business community as well.

But Kansas was proud of its frontier independence and bitterly resentful of anything that Washington did. The result was that they refused to take part in program after program offered by Franklin Roosevelt to carry through the readjustment period. Most of the relief programs were ignored. Social security was resisted (none of the schools or municipal offices were permitted to take part in retirement funds or credit unions) and the major employers refused any assistance offered through government loans or subsidy programs. They left their businesses closed or three-fourths laid off, but they did very little complaining either.

The result was that the unemployment problem in Wichita was probably unnecessarily severe and certainly lasted longer than most communities of over 100,000 population. There was an extraordinary number of jobless, literally without any support whatsoever.

Strangely enough, the only official in the community who dared resist this trend was Alfred MacDonald. While on the one hand he was probably the most conservative citizen in City Hall, at the same time he saw the opportunity for greatly improving his park system through the federal programs. The result was that during most of the worst of the Depression, the only WPA and NYA jobs in the city were in the Park Department. With a cold-blooded opportunism, matched with an unknown amount of humanitarianism, he bulled one project after another through the City Commissioners and the business community, and proceeded to upgrade his parks. He built an airport with PWA funds that was twenty years ahead of its time. He drained the river, rip-rapped its walls for four miles on either side, then refilled it for regattas and motorboating. He built an art museum (and left it vacant till maintenance funds might appear). He put in tennis courts, picnic grounds, more swimming pools, stone shelters, a day camp, and miles of walks and nature trails. The federal programs were limited to capital improvements, so there was no money to staff or care for his expansions, but the physical plant was upgraded throughout while most of the other civic services—indeed the town itself—seemed to be decaying.

By the late Thirties, the town had begun to recover and there was hope again that it was going to survive. By this time, much of MacDonald's programs were well along—but in fairness to him, he was desperately short of funds just to keep the grass mowed and the parks clean. Father's enthusiasm for park programs and tournaments and extravaganzas coincided with MacDonald's improvements, so as soon as MacDonald would open a new facility, Father would lock it into a fury of activity using a highly complex system of volunteer help. He had the high schools staging the water carnivals on the reconstructed river. He had Little Theater groups donating their time in plays which moved from one park amphitheater to another. He had intercity sports tournaments sponsored by the various service clubs. In all of the excitement, he and MacDonald were in a grudging accord—except with the zoo. MacDonald considered it a colossal waste of time and money, and Father considered it the emerald in the crown of park activities. Spring was at hand, and he was going forward with his plans come hell or h. w.

The first I heard about it developed in our garage on a Saturday morning, when Father, Jim, and Bob Saylor all convened to look over the winterized pets.

"I think the time to push this thing off will be the week after Easter," Father was saying. "They'll be painting up and cleaning around and there's sure to've been some winter losses. I think if we hit 'em just when they're beginning to shape things up for spring we'll have our best chance."

"Do you actually know they've got an extra lioness, or are you just hoping?", Saylor asked.

"No, no, they've got a lioness that's surplus. The only thing is, will they give her to *us?*" Father replied. "Here's the situation so far: I wrote them saying that we needed a young lioness, and that we had some good black bears and some other things and would they be interested. They said they could use two bears and they could spare a lioness. They didn't actually say so in so many words, but they implied there were a number of other bidders for her, though, and they as much as asked what else did we have to offer?"

"How much more do you think it'll take?"

"Well, Trefflich's lists young lions for twice as much as the bears would bring. This leaves us way short, but maybe we can scare up enough odds and ends so we can interest them with variety."

"You going to ask 'em again?"

"No. It seemed to me if we put it all down on paper it'd seem pretty pitiful. But if we sailed right up to them with the stuff it'd look more impressive."

"You mean take the stuff down there without knowing if they'll take it?"

"That's what I was thinking, yes."

"What if they just laugh and say go away?"

"That's a chance we'll have to take, but it's always possible they won't. And if they do, we'll just have to turn around and come home."

"How far is it to Oklahoma City?"

"Hundred and seventy-five miles," Father said.

"Four or five hours with the truck. You'd have a time getting back the same day," Saylor pointed out in truth.

"We could make it. We might have to run a bit after dark, but we could get back."

"I think you're building yourself up to get insulted, if you ask me," said Saylor. "Does MacDonald know about this?"

"Well, I've told him I was negotiating with Oklahoma City about taking some of our surplus."

"Didn't mention the lion, huh?"

"It seemed to me that if they refused, there was no sense in getting him all worked up, and if we happened to get away with it, I could suggest that they made the offer and it was too good to pass up."

"Well, it's you funeral, not mine—I hope," said Saylor.

"All right," Father concluded. "Let's see what we can put together to convince them."

Right off the bat, my mother caught it. The week before Easter—two weeks before The Great Day—Father pulled the pin.

"Mae, we've decided to take a couple hundred goldfish with us on the trip."

"Where are you going to get them, Bernie?"

"Jim thinks that if we dip a couple dozen out of each pool, it'll add up to what we need without thinning our own parks too much."

"How are you going to move them?"

"We're going to load 'em in twenty-gallon milk cans and put them on the truck. The Fish and Game Department thinks they'll make it if they don't have to stay in the cans too long."

"Where are you going to collect them?"

"Well, Mae, that was what I was getting to. We need a place we can bring a few every day, and yet we've got to have them so they can be loaded fast when we roll out. That way they'll be in the cans the shortest possible time. All the ponds have lilies in 'em and mud bottoms. I think we're going to have to keep them in the bathtub here at home."

"Oh, you wouldn't dare do such a thing! I won't have them in the house—and where would *we* bathe, for Heaven's sake?"

"What are you complaining about? They're clean, you know! They're bathing all the time! No, Mae. We need some place we can aerate and then empty quickly. We'll let the water run hard and it'll keep the bubbles churning and they'll be fully oxygenated when we load them—they'll be all ready to go when we need to scoop 'em out."

So we began to accumulate goldfish in the bathtub. Outdoor goldfish have to be a certain size to make good display material. They have to be large enough and plump enough to be seen from the side of a water-lily pond, but they have to be below the carp stage when a goldfish begins to lose his color and "pet-shape" and starts looking like a cold, half-dead scavenger. This forced a good deal of dipping and throwing back. The technique involved was for Jim and a WPA helper to approach a pool and lay a large sheet of white oilcloth out on the sidewalk by the side of the water. The oilcloth was latticed with black lines making eight-inch squares over the surface. The helper would wade out in the pool with a triangular-shaped dip net and start scraping from one side to the other. This would collect thirty or forty fish of all sizes and shapes, and he would then dump the fish out on the oilcloth.

The fish would flop around and gradually sort themselves out. When the heaps were distributed out to one deep, Jim would dip his hand in water and start picking up the ones that were within an inch or so of the eight-inch squares. He'd toss these into a waiting pail of pool water and when he'd grabbed everything that looked appropriate, he'd pick up the oilcloth like a bedsheet and dump everything back into the pond. The fish could stay out as long as three or four minutes without being hurt. The only flaw in this method was that as the dipping net was worked back and forth, it caught some of the same fish over and over again. Nevertheless, in three-quarters of an hour, Jim would have accumulated two or three pailfuls of the six- to ten-inch variety, and they'd suspend operations. He would then lay a board over each pail, load it into the small truck, and head for our house. Once there, Jim would diffidently knock on the back door, and Mother would open it. The men would tiptoe across the kitchen, down the hall to the bathroom, and dump the buckets into the bathtub. The tub would already be full with the water spewing in to make bubbles and the overflow running out the upper drain. The pail water would fill the tub to the very edge and then subside just before it slopped over the side. Mother watched the operation each time in icy silence, and neither of the men would speak a word. In this manner, we accumulated 250 to 300 goldfish.

I thought the whole affair was a ball and dragged my friends in to see the things to Mother's great distress. I would have supposed that such crowding would have killed the specimens right and left, but I don't recall losing more than two or three which I hurriedly flushed down the plumbing before Mother noticed. I fed them every evening when I came home from school, dumping in two or three cupfuls of dry oatmeal. The churning they would set up over these late afternoon feedings made the place look alive and gave it a sort of grotesque, obscene activity with the fish kneading themselves into swirls. It was both fascinating and repellent to watch.

In the meantime, Father had everybody available constructing crates of various sizes. The two big crates for the bears were made massively of two-by-fours and spikes, reinforced in all directions so if the truck got involved in an accident, they would resist any chance of cracking open and releasing the occupants. The crates were deliberately made large enough so that either one could accommodate a young lion, if Father was successful. In addition to these, he made boxes for all sorts of animals and birds, each one with appropriate wire across one open side and a piece of burlap hanging down over the wire like a curtain. The ones destined to hold small animals were accumulated at the zoo, the ones for birds were put together and stacked at home in front of the garage. Easter came and went with the family maintaining the proper Methodist activities of the season—preparatory bathing for each being done out of the sinks throughout the house.

Came the final days before departure. The cages were finished, the bathtub was brimming, and the smell of spring was in the air. Father was hanging everything on a psychological assault. He had remembered the impact the pet deluge had had on him. It wasn't any single specimen which had shaken us; it was the sight of little squirming things everywhere you looked. He hoped that gross variety would make up for the questionable value of his bid.

The Wednesday following Easter arrived and the morning dawned warmish but cloudy. A mixed blessing. The smell of spring was there, but a good rain would bedraggle even the healthiest animals. They decided to proceed as planned.

I held off from my first class to the last minute to see the preparations for departure. The zoo truck arrived at our house at 8:30 and slowly backed into our driveway, headed for the garage. It was one of the big Park Department trucks with a wide, flat bed and high stake sides. It already looked impressive.

The two bear crates were anchored in the center, with ropes guying them to the sides. The bears could be seen pacing back and forth within. Down each side and across the open end were stout box-cages with all sorts of live things showing. In various places were six different boxes, each holding a bright-eyed cayman. There were two albino possums in together. A fat raccoon could be seen through the wire of another. Father was giving up—and prominently displaying—a full-grown spider monkey. In other crates, wired beside, around, and over the others were pheasants of various varieties, and a net had been thrown over the whole arrangement and a peacock turned loose to hop around at large. True to his plan, there seemed to be eyes peeking out everywhere, and all kinds of shapes in evidence.

Once the truck was firmly stopped, everyone began swarming over it, working as rapidly as possible. Four empty, 20-gallon milk cans were lugged through the kitchen and into the bathroom. Jim and a helper I'd never even seen before started working with two white enamel pails, and began bailing the tub, scooping water and fish and pouring the stuff into the milk cans. They got most of the water in, and all of the fish. The two men then lugged the cans back outdoors, one at a time, and tied them on the running boards of the truck, wiring them to hinges and mirrors and door handles, so the fish were solid, but the only way you could get into the cab was through the windows. They filled up the remaining space in each can with a garden hose, and clamped on the lids.

In the meantime, everyone else was catching birds, putting them into the crates, and wiring the crates to the outside of the truck sides. This made the truck about three feet wider than the regulations permitted, but this detail was the least of Father's worries. By the time they had finished, the effect was everything he could have hoped for. The truck looked like a massive, mound of squirming wildlife, and the colorful birds on the outside—I caught glimpses of cockatiels, and parrots, and finches, indeed everything that could possibly be considered surplus as well as specimens I was astonished he was parting with—all adding up to a sort of calliope-merry-go-round-traveling zoo effect.

Just before I had to leave for school, Peterson drove up in the Park patrol car and got out, carrying an enormous game rifle. As I pedalled away on my bicycle, they were helping him into the cab through the right window.

Late that night, Father returned with the news.

It seemed they had rolled with Saylor driving the truck, Peterson in the middle with the rifle (which, it developed, was for shooting either the bears or the hoped-for lion, if any accidentally escaped), and Father by the right window. Loaded as they were, they had to accelerate and decelerate with great deliberation for fear both of hurting some of the specimens or dislodging some of the cages. They required considerable time to get through Wichita, and then created a continual traffic jam on the highway toward Oklahoma. The truck would roll along at a solid forty miles an hour, with the wind lifting up the burlap curtains, revealing the occupants in bursts. Whenever the oncoming lanes would be clear, a number of the cars accumulated behind would come swooping around to pass, suddenly realize what all the mess on the truck was, and go careening from road to shoulder and back, trying to see it all as they went past. Once out in front, they would drive for a half a mile either watching through the rear vision mirror or actually sticking their heads out the windows and looking back. The result was that the truck was lumbering along, and cars behind it, beside it, and in front of it were zigzagging all over the highway. The men in the cab sat there helplessly watching potential accidents build up, get averted at the last minute, just in time for another one to develop. The nerve strain was exhausting.

About thirty miles south of Wichita, the clouds condensed out and they got a steady, drenching spring rain, complete with typical prairie thunder and lightning. The men shuddered to think what must be happening behind them, but as long as it rained there seemed little they could do about it, so they drove on while it poured. About ten miles south of Wellington (40 miles south of Wichita), the sky finally stopped falling, but the pyrotechnics kept flashing and thundering. With everything dripping, they pulled off the road into a highway maintenance turnoff, and fell out through the windows to see what damage had been done to the load. Everyone was crawling around, peeking into crates, and pulling soaked burlap back into place, when it occurred to Father that this would be a good time to aerate the goldfish for a few minutes. He therefore proceeded to loosen the tops of the milk cans—at precisely the moment a bolt of lightning hit the utility pole beside the truck. I have heard the story of that blast at least three dozen times from each of the men, so often it seems like I was there myself.

Apparently the charge hit the pole, supercharged the atmosphere around it, with some of it bursting the pole and going straight down into the ground, other portions rolling in round balls of flames in both directions down the barbed wire fence behind the pole—and a minor fragment jumping toward the goldfish can which Father was working on, hands wet and feet in the soaked gravel. It knocked him flat on his back, fully conscious, with a minimum of discomfort, simply stretched out on the ground. Both the men rushed around to see what had happened and he struggled to his feet, with the top of the milk can still in his right hand. Much trying of joints and feeling around, but no apparent damage anywhere. Once they'd checked out Father, they abandoned further activities and crawled back into the truck and continued south. The skies began to clear and the wind began to dry everything aboard in a rush.

About one-thirty they arrived in Oklahoma City, had a quick lunch on the outskirts (generating a satisfyingly large throng in the parking lot), and proceeded to the zoo—tying up traffic all through the town.

Once in the zoo, they proceeded to the Administration Building and introduced themselves. The Oklahoma City Zoo was then, and still is, a splendid series of displays. Built with oil money in great chunks, it goes in big for barless, moated outdoor displays, but has extensive indoor exhibits as well. The various supervisors began to accumulate around the truck, followed by keepers and the public, till it was the center of a substantial crowd. In the midst of all this, Father was spraying words, flipping up burlap curtains, pointing with pride, and weaving a threnody about his problems at home.

In short, whether from conviction, or confusion, or out of pity at the spectacle, the Oklahomans graciously accepted all the odds and ends, cleared the truck, and Father returned triumphant with his lioness. It had come off just as he had said it would—though to this day, no one is just sure why.

By early dusk they had the truck cleared, and the young lioness back inside one of the empty bear crates. Father expressed a profuse and genuine gratitude for their generosity and the three men headed back north, this time with the empty milk cans and cages tightly stored in the truck bed. Once it was dark, they constituted less of a road hazard, but the shock to the common driver was still evident. A car would come roaring down the highway, overtake the truck and start to sweep around it, when its headlights would pick up the lioness. The car would waver back and forth and then cut back behind the truck again, braking down furiously, but determined to see if it really was what it looked like. Once they were assured they weren't cracking up, they'd honk merrily and pass around.

By ten o'clock they were at Riverside Zoo, and by midnight the cleaning cage was occupied with our new guest. Father then returned home and we got the story for the first time.

In the course of the week that followed, the three lions got to know each other through the bars, and then during a warm afternoon Simba was driven into his outdoor cage for the first time of the season, and the young lioness (still unnamed) was passed through Simba's cage into young King's. They got along famously from the very beginning and within an hour Simba was permitted back in, where he sulked for two days.

The lioness trade set the pattern for the rest of the spring. Every few weeks Saylor and Charlie Peterson would load up a bear or two and head out to make an exchange—though these were always worked out by mail and agreed on ahead of time.

They rolled over to Independence and brought back a pair of mule deer. They traded a bear for a pair of bison that Bartlesville, Oklahoma, had as surplus. The Colorado Springs zoo had an elk that was tradeable, but they had no use for any more black bears. If either we or they could find someone who wanted a bear, who in turn had something Colorado Springs could use, Father could negotiate.

And so it went. As each of the new animals arrived, the papers gave it the usual coverage, and before long the town began to get a slight touch of zoo fever. Like Lincoln Steffens' synthetic crime wave, it seemed to the glazed reader that the zoo must be a veritable beehive of activity. More people came out to see, larger crowds themselves gave a heightened air of drama. Father began to run short of bears, and the feathered "we'll throw in a few——, if you like," were completely gone.

Father suddenly found himself short of anything to give away, just when things were coming in so well. He needed some zoological loosc change. It forced him to creative thinking.

# 9

# *The Dog Census*

"I've got it! I've got it! Here's the answer to the problem!" Father came storming in one evening waving a four-color brochure. He flung it down on the dining table, not yet set for supper, and pointed dramatically, "That's going to keep us in business!"

I picked up the pamphlet and read, "Tired of Looking for Game? Why Not Raise Your Own? Stock Your Favorite Hunting Land Yourself!" It was a cheerful little item with a picture of a well-fed bobwhite and a ringneck on the cover and inside a prettily illustrated sequence of how you too could grow game birds without trouble or expense. The book had been prepared (and was being distributed) by a St. Louis feed and grain dealer who assured us that all one needed for overwhelming success in this endeavor was a few hundred pounds of his miracle turkey mash. Just fill up the feed trays and jump back. The mash would do all the rest.

The dealer, who must have been stuck with some of last year's crop, had combined the texts of a half dozen fish and game department pamphlets and had come up with this grow-them-yourself idea. He described in simple, well-illustrated steps how the chicks developed from egg to winged flight, ending with a hunting party in a cornfield blasting away at a skyful of birds.

I riffled through the pages while Father smiled triumphantly. It was not coming through to me as clearly as for Father.

"You're going to raise bobwhites for hunters?" I asked stupidly.

"No, no, no. It's the pheasants. It says there you can grow your own. If you can grow ringnecks, you can grow Reeves, and Amhersts, and goldens. And if you can grow Reeves and goldens, you can grow peacocks and jungle fowl. And why not mallards, and teal, and wood ducks? I think we can go into the ornamental bird business and keep marketable, tradeable stuff coming along as fast as we need it. We could've used ten times as many peacocks as we had. Nobody's raising peacocks. All you ever see are occasional extras. Why don't we?"

"By 'we,' do you mean the zoo?"

"No. You can do it this summer. Right here at home. We can put the incubator in the basement, and you can build some brooders in the back yard while the first hatch is coming off, and by fall we'll have enough to work with."

"Mother'll have a fit," I pointed out. This also looked like work, and though I was resigned to having to make some money for freshman tuition next fall, I had pictured something more negotiable than wood ducklings.

"Look, the incubator'll be inside, and nobody'll know about it. The brooder houses won't have to be too big, and as soon as the birds get big enough to make it on their own, we'll move them into the big pens at the zoo. It'll be good experience for you."

At the time, I was planning to be an American History professor, so the vocational advantages were not so clear as they might have been.

"Isn't this incubator business pretty tricky? Can we run one without any experience?" I was groping for an out.

"This pamphlet says that's the easiest part. All you do is set it for the right temperature, turn the eggs a couple of times a day, and the egg does the rest."

"Where'll we get the eggs?"

"The Game Department will give us some. I've checked. We can pick up plenty from our own stock—instead of just throwing them away like we do now. And if we promise to give 'em some of the hatch, I'm sure we can get Independence, Hutchinson, and Great Bend to send us whatever they get. Maybe we can even get some from Denver and K.C. That's not going to be any problem."

"Have you got an incubator?"

"No, but I'm going over to Monkey Wards tomorrow and see what they run."

THAT was the problem.

They ran from $150 up. And in a day when new Chevrolets sold for $800, "$150" was like saying "$600 and up," today. I had won my reprieve.

April and May passed and Father read that grow-your-own-birds book over and over again. His disappointment was agonizing to watch, and before I realized it, I'd lowered my guard and let myself in for as strange a slice of nonsense as I've ever stumbled into: the bureaucracy gone wild.

It began in my Government class. The teacher announced that he had ten jobs in the City government which had been made available as a sort of "internship" to young high school graduates, and he was going to offer them to us. Some would only run a few weeks and others all summer. He could not guarantee which we'd get, but if we wanted a close-up opportunity of seeing government at work, this was our chance. In a burst of generosity which astonished even me, I decided I would take one of the short jobs and give Father whatever I made so he could at least make a down payment on his incubator.

With this in mind, I conned a fellow student and friend by the name of Al Munroe into joining me in the adventure; and came the Monday after graduation, we headed for the City Building. The question was less, What is the job?, but more, How much does it pay?

With this foremost in our minds, we reported in at the Personnel Office, filled out an unbelievable number of forms, and then were given a card instructing us where to proceed for our assignment. To our astonishment, it was a two-chair barbershop over by the Union Station, in the somewhat seedier part of town.

We went there. We entered perplexed and introduced

ourselves and were told to sit down in the chairs along the mirror and wait. In time four more youths of our age arrived and the first-chair barber addressed us with an orientation lecture.

"Boys, you're about to take a dog census. I'm gonna give you a bunch of slips of paper, and every time you find a dog and can get the name and address of the guy he belongs to, you'll get ten cents. Don't think you can kid me, see, because I've been running these things ever' four years since before you was born. Ever' one of the papers is got a number on it, and I expect to get ever' one back, see? And don't go making up names, hear? Now, you got two weeks to do the job in. You'll get your money at the end, but you come in here ever' day or so and I'll give you some more slips and some more streets. I'll give you slips and streets as fast as you need 'em, but you hit ever' house, see, and don't think you can kid me, because . . ." et cetera.

Monroe and I were to work as a team. Each one of us would take one side of a street, the streets to be assigned four at a time, running from city limit to city limit. The assault was to begin the next morning and continue for fourteen days; how far and how fast we would go were up to us.

We signed for our numbered pads and carbon paper, and left, somewhat mystified, but intrigued at the possibilities of the operation. It was just barely possible we had stumbled on to a gold mine here. Most of our friends were taking summer jobs in stores at $16.50 a week or on construction projects for $20. To match their $16.50 would require 165 dogs apiece. Surely in a week we could each find 165 dogs;

but how did you find out whose they were? And just how would the owners react to the official presentation prescribed by our leader? We looked to the next morning with mild concern.

Following an early breakfast, we took a bus to the southern extremity of town, walked two blocks to the limit of our first assigned street, and started toward the other end, five miles to the north. Elm-shaded and peaceful, it looked like an early summer *Saturday Evening Post* cover. I took the west side, and Munroe the east. Pursuing instructions to the letter, I went up the walk of the first house, mounted the porch, and knocked at the door. The sound of a chair being pushed back was followed by the head of the house approaching in undershirt and pants. He peered through the screen door and said, "Yeah?"

I lifted the pad and pencil to present arms and declared, as instructed, "Good morning, sir. I'm from the police department, and we're taking a dog census. Is there a dog in this household?"

"The hell you say," he said.

"Yes, sir. What I mean is, do you have a dog here, sir?"

"You're kidding, huh?"

"No! No sir. You don't have a dog, I suppose?"

"A dog census! Hah! I'll be damned. A dog census. How about that? A dog census . . ." By this time he'd turned around and disappeared into the house, leaving me peering through the screen.

I turned around myself and walked back toward the street, where I found Munroe already waiting. "Did yours have one?" I asked.

"I don't think so."

"What'd they say?"

"I'm not sure. I don't think they were up yet, and the lady was pretty short."

We reversed our fields and looked at the next houses on our respective sides. The thing was even more complicated than we'd thought, and we were both nearly as scared of finding a dog as we were of being laughed at. The real threat to the program was our little pad of paper slips, yellow ones for the householders and white receipts for the barber, carbons in between. The slips read:

City of Wichita, Kansas

*To:* (name)

*Of:* (address)

Summons

You are hereby ordered to appear in Police Court within five days to receive sentence for failure to secure dog license. Sentence shall not exceed thirty days nor fifty dollars fine. Such action may be forestalled by the payment of $2.00 (male) or $3.50 (female) each to license all dogs found in your custody. Such payment may be made at the Department of Licenses, City Hall, from 9:00 to 5:00, Monday through Saturday.

It had quickly become apparent to all of us, even back in the barbershop, that the word "census" was at best a euphemism. One of the others had asked the barber if this notice might not pique some of the citizens, and he had replied, with a strange smile, "Yep! Some of 'em get a bit exercised all right."

Munroe had asked, "What if they've already licensed the dog? Shouldn't we ask them before we fill out the slip?"

And the barber had replied, "Nope. Ain't hardly anybody has, so it ain't likely you'll run into 'em. If you ask 'em if they've got a license, they'll all say they have, and you'll never have no excuse for filling out the slip and shoving it on 'em. You only get paid on the slip, you know. If they scream and yell too loud after you give it to 'em, you can tell 'em that the license bureau will check 'em all, and if they really have paid, they can forget it. You won't hardly ever find anybody who has, so you needn't worry—much." Even at the time, the slight hesitation in his otherwise forthright delivery had disturbed us.

I climbed the porch of the second house. Much knocking. Nobody home. Went up to the third house. A grandmotherly-looking lady came out, and I tried the official approach. She looked puzzled, decided she had misunderstood, started to ask again, and decided against it. "No," she said, and shut the door. I abandoned porch three for porch four.

Or, rather, stoop four. This house had the look of belonging to a carpenter or someone in the building trade. It had no porch, but had a fan-shaped brick and concrete veranda and a neat, newly painted doorway. Everything about the place looked alert and well cared for. I pressed the doorbell and precipitated a peal of chimes inside. A large man of about fifty came to the door with a massive hound of some variety beside him. The beast woofed a couple of times and looked curiously at me through the screen door.

"Good morning, sir," I recited. "I'm from the police department, and we're taking a dog census. I see you have one there! Ha, ha, ha." Striking the man-to-man approach.

"You betcha, son. This is George. George is just like one of the family. He's three years old, and I'll swear he's still growing."

"He's a good one, all right!" I tried to keep it friendly and nonchalant. "Let's see now, let me make a note of this. This is 3639 South Topeka, isn't it? And your name, sir, is . . . ?"

"Alexander Strean. S-t-r-e-a-n."

"Thank you, sir. Here's this little slip of paper, and thank you for your courtesy." He opened the screen door, took the paper, and began to read. His face clouded as he progressed.

"Go get him, George," he said in a flat voice, and the dog scrambled past him and shot out the open door with a machine-gun like roar of barks, growls, and woofs all mixed together. His ears were down and his hair up.

I backed down the steps as fast as I could go without falling over backward, and as I treadled toward where the street must be, I could remember that the secret of dealing with either dogs or horses was not to let them know you were afraid. So, as I staggered backward, I fixed the hound with what I hoped was a stern expression and wheezed, "Now, George. Down, boy. Down, George! Stop it, boy. Down, George. Down! Down!"

At this moment I found the street, fell over the curb, and landed in a skidding arc on my back. I wrenched forward to protect myself against the expected lunge and was startled to find George, with his front feet precisely on the edge of the grass in front of the curb, laying down a barrage of noise but not moving an inch. I had just learned the first great truth on which we built the next two weeks: If You Can Make It to the Nearest Property Line, You Are in the Clear.

By this time, Munroe had rushed over to help me up, and we stood there in the street, brooding on the situation. In one block we had both been lied to, and I had been assaulted. The time had come to make up our minds. Either we were going to abandon the whole thing or mount a major, formal campaign. We weighed pride, limbs, the authority of the state, and ten cents a dog in the balance and decided to give battle. The first thing we had to have was arms.

We retraced our steps to the bus line and rode back downtown to an office supply store. We entered and asked to see their selection of clipboards—the larger the better. They produced a choice that exceeded our wildest hopes. Munroe invested the equivalent of twenty dogs in a doubled aluminum job which was about the size of a snow shovel (it was intended as a wallboard for an automobile parts department), and I sank fifteen dogs' worth in a massive wooden model which was as thick as my thumb and weighed well over three pounds. It was capped with a huge steel clip on top and two mounting hinges on the back, which gave it a beautiful heft. We stood there in the store practicing knee-high sweeps with these, like golf pros selecting a set of woods. In the ensuing days we became marvelously skilled with these weapons. My backhand was always my best. I could sweep that board from a writing position down, across, and up the side of the head of a charging chow or schnauzer like Manolete in his prime. With little snapping terriers and bulldogs, a fast wrist action not unlike a sculling stroke over the stern of a rowboat permitted me to back to the property line with complete aplomb, leaving the dogs breathless and faintly confused as to their bearings.

Munroe maintained his dignity throughout. His metal board would drop from chest high with a single firm forehand, catching boxers and German shepherds across the skull, between the ears. A momentary opacity would cross their eyes, and you could almost hear their heads ringing. By the time they were in focus and ready to spring, Munroe would have withdrawn to the next lot, walking backward with all the assurance of the chancellor leaving the Queen.

We snapped our little pads into our new boards and headed back for South Topeka Street. From there on, we abandoned the official approach and developed our own. If the householder was a young woman, we played the rueful innocent: "Lady, you aren't going to believe this, but the city is paying us ten cents for any dog we can find. Do you have a dog?" When she had finished laughing and admitted she *did* have a little specimen in the garage, we'd say, "Now, some knothead at City Hall has written up the worst possible way of reminding you, but this is supposed to be a notice telling you it's time to get a dog license. Just ignore what it says, but get downtown before too long and get everybody off your neck." With this approach we wouldn't get the dog sicked on us more than three times out of five.

Elderly ladies never understood what we were doing no matter how we phrased it. We finally got so we abandoned all formality, and when one would open the door we'd just say, "Good morning, ma'am, do you have a dog?" If she would say yes, we would ask her name, fill out the slip, fold it, and hand it to her closed over, saying, "Please give this to your husband when he comes home. Thank you."

All men under fifty arrived at the door mad before they even knew what we wanted, so we snapped out our question as nastily as they had saluted us, and although we would get the dog after us five times out of five, we at least retained our pride.

In this manner we worked our way up and down the streets of Wichita. We would start off at seven-thirty in the morning and keep at it till nine at night, when we would take a late bus home, tender of knuckle and leg-weary. Inasmuch as we were backing out of about one yard in three, we not only found muscles we had never noticed, we were wearing out soles faster than heels. But we did find dogs. To this day I stand in amazement at the way they appeared everywhere in every size and shape. By the end of the first day, I had flushed out over a hundred and eighty specimens and had netted eighteen dollars for the day. This beat grading papers or sacking groceries all hollow.

In the ensuing days, we increased our unit production as

well. We found that if you scuffed your feet on the way to the porch, whistled loudly, and rattled the screen door ever so slightly before knocking on it, you could rouse the family dog to a fury long before the householder could swear he had never had a pet of any kind. Similarly, we found we could increase our efficiency by locating the neighborhood grouch. She would give herself away at once by snapping, "No, I don't have a dog, and the city ought to shoot every one they find. The least people could do is to keep theirs tied up." To this we would reply, all innocence, "Oh, is there one next door?"

This would usually elicit, "No, not them, but the next ones down have a big nasty one that's always in my roses. Then the people in that yellow house there have two that run loose all day." Having sold out her fellowman, she felt better, and we could head directly to pay dirt.

Everything seemed to be going well for the first few days, and although Munroe inexplicably found about fifteen percent more dogs on his side of the street than I did, there were plenty for all, and we progressed block after block through the city, spreading interruption and fury as we went. We stopped washing machines, telephone calls, baths, lawn mowers, vacuum sweepers, and infant feedings. As I look back now, it is a miracle we weren't lynched.

By the second week, however, our daily haul, which had been climbing nicely, began to decline. Not only did we find fewer dogs, but people seemed less and less astonished to be interviewed regarding a dog census. It soon became clear that the three small teams, although apparently lost in a town of 115,000, were beginning to be known. Ruth had phoned Margaret, who had warned the Pattersons, and by the time we arrived, all we got was the lady of the house looking us straight in the eye and saying, "We've never had a dog," with the nine-year-old whispering from the kitchen, "Hold her a little longer—he's still here."

By the time we made our final trip back to the barber shop, I had recorded 1,650 dogs and Munroe had identified 1,948. I remember to the penny the $165.00 and the $194.80 we took in. It was fifteen years and a World War later before I again made so much money for two weeks' work.

But I had bought Father one red mahogany 600-egg incubator, free and clear, all express and delivery charges paid for.

# 10

# *The Incubator*

Suddenly the incubator became the axis on which the household spun. Even before its arrival—when it was still just a page in an order book—it began to rip things from their moorings. The first to go was the house itself.

Father had spent too long brooding on that hatch-'em-yourself booklet. Having nothing to absorb his energy, he had built imaginary brooders and holding pens and feed rooms in his mind, and had soon come to the conclusion that our present house "wasn't arranged right to get the best possible use out of the machine." While Mother might be satisfied with our proper neighborhood, Father felt it frustrated his coming potential. To think was to act. As the spring had progressed, he'd kept a sharp eye out while driving through the city on official business, and ultimately he'd spotted the house he needed. With the incubator converted from the possible to the really coming, Mother and I found ourselves in the front yard of an empty house only two blocks from the University (and some five miles from our own home).

Father gave us the lecture and we soon learned that this was the Babb House—the home of one of the founding families of Wichita—where an ex-mayor had lived for the past twenty years. The final member of the family had recently passed on and the property was up for sale.

"Mae, this will put you right down the street from the University, and you can walk to the library and plays and concerts and the lecture series. It'll be ideal."

I would be a freshman on the campus in four months, so its advantages to me were obvious.

"And Chuck, if the incubator idea works out, we can set up brooder pens in the side yard, and a row of holding pens clear across the back. The lot's a hundred-fifty feet wide, you see. They kept the lot beside it and made it into a garden. You line your pens on the side lawn, and Mother can keep up the flowers around the borders. There's an outside entrance to the basement, so we can get the incubator in and keep it cared for without bothering Mother. You can see, it's ideal."

In fact, it was. The house sat on a corner intersection, separated from the nearest neighbor by a hundred feet in every direction, and if the surrounding faculty and gracious homeowners would let him bring in the fauna, he was right. There were so many things going for it that both Mother's and my natural conservatism were undermined, and completely ignoring the fact that the whole thing was designed to make the incubator feel at home, we agreed on the spot. By the time the machine arrived, we had moved, were in the "new house" (it was twenty years older than the "old" one, but considerably larger), and the incubator was delivered into the new basement. It sat there on the dry, dusty, concrete floor, silent and smelling of wood and furniture polish. It looked capable, efficient, and forbidding.

The machine which was soon to break me to serfdom was about the size of a large refrigerator laid on its side, with a mahogany exterior, and a single door in the "front end." The door had a glass window in it, and you could see two thermometers inside, facing out through the gloom. On the top there was a bright red light bulb, and rows of holes the size of bottle tops scattered about. The bulb was obviously to tell whether the thing was on, and the holes all had little sliding brass covers, presumably to control the ventilation inside. A crisply illustrated booklet lay on top, and the night the incubator arrived, I leaned against the nearby workbench and began to read. Within three pages I could see we were over our heads.

I had assumed that the idea of an incubator was to keep the eggs warm. I supposed that if you cooked them gently for some length of time, whatever was supposed to be inside would fill up and pop out. This proved to be the least of the problem. Most of the machine's effort was to duplicate that natural churning a hen makes on a nest, and (you'll excuse the expression) the perspiration she puts into it. It's the subtle "humidity" which comes hard. It seemed the machine was going to struggle to get just the sublime dampness which an egg would feel if sat upon by a poorly ventilated hen, resting on the moist ground, beneath a sparse bush, subject to a heavy rain every five days. The text convinced me this would be no mean feat.

But we were going after it scientifically. It developed that inside, immediately above the glass door, there was an electric fan facing the opposite end of the box. When the fan blew, the wind ran the length of the machine and hit a curved vane which directed it downwards, it then blew to the bottom, hit another vane bending it back toward the front. Beneath the door a third curve got it back up the front—into the fan again. We were going to have active air if nothing else.

About six inches above the bottom of the incubator there was a long, zinc tray suspended in space. This was about two inches deep and as wide as the machine and was clearly designed to hold water. The instructions made it plain that once the door was shut and the fan was turned on, the air would blow across the pan, pick up moisture, blow past the hygrometer in the window, hit the fan, and go roaring around again. The hatcher was supposed to watch the hygrometer at regular intervals to see how moist things were getting. If it was too wet, he opened a few of the little holes in the top a bit; too dry, close things up tighter, and he was supposed to keep fiddling around until he found the Elysian combination of hot water and fresh air. Apparently there was no worry about its getting much too dry so long as you kept the door closed and the tray filled. As it later proved, I could handle the door part, but the water in the tray was murder.

Under the tray there were great, black coils of bare metal

which, when the switch was on, glowed red and gave off the heat required to "keep the temperature up." This phrase was repeated constantly, and the disasters tied to "chilling" made the blood run cold. It seemed that the temperature of various birds was slightly different. A mother duck gave off 99 degrees. A ringneck pheasant, 101. And our game birds had a collection of heats that fell in the 98 to 102 range. Since we were going to have various kinds of eggs in the thing, I wondered just how critical the degrees were, and if it was possible to convince the eggs that "this was an unusually cool summer"—or whatever was required to account for the discrepancies. The thermometer behind the window was extraordinarily official looking, with very small lines and very silver mercury, which required weaving back and forth on your knees to read. A thermostat inside was supposed to keep the temperature you wanted, but the fact that it took two pages to explain how to adjust it was ominous in itself.

The whole idea of the incubator was to make a home for the eggs, of course, and so it had been equipped accordingly. The center of the thing was filled with six trays, wooden sides and wire bottoms, which slid in on runners and which were suspended in air behind the glass. They ran the whole length of the machine. Having reached this part in the instructions, I whipped open the door dramatically, and was startled to have the thermometer and hygrometer swing out into the room behind it. It turned out these were properly anchored to the rear of the door in brackets, so I progressed and cautiously pulled out one of the empty trays. I'd assumed I'd find a bare, wire box. Not so. Instead, there were neat wire egg holders marching row upon row, each one just the size of some variety of shell, and each one hinged on a little pivot so the egg could be tilted back and forth.

Back to the instructions, and it was revealed that I was expected to change the lean of the egg every eight hours, day and night, for three and a half weeks. This, it was explained, would duplicate the rolling of an egg in the nest and permit the chick to develop smoothly in all directions. If an egg were permitted to lie in any one position too long, it would settle to the side and the author didn't dare tell us what disasters that would reap. The little egg holders went from the plump to the middle-sized to the tiny. Being a game bird hatchery, the designer had cleverly provided comfort for turkey and peacock eggs (large), partridge and pheasant eggs (medium), and quail eggs (very small). Six wire tray covers were identified as lying beneath the water tray, and I dug them out and leaned them against the work bench. These could be fitted over the trays after the chicks got large enough to require some confinement. With everything accounted for, parts F-1, W-4, T-2, et cetera, properly located and messed with, I felt there was nothing more to do until we got the eggs.

Father was lining these up all over central Kansas. He had a rancher promising him a dozen golden pheasant eggs here, and the Bartlesville Zoo six Amherst eggs there. The State Fish and Game Hatchery at Pratt promised us a hundred ringneck and forty mutants (provided we would come to get them), and Father had Jim and Bob Saylor watching the cages at Riverside like hawks.

When late spring arrived, the zoo birds proceeded to lay eggs just as deliberately as setting hens in a barn, even though there was nothing in their cages that even looked like a nest. When an egg was formed, the hen would deposit it wherever she happened to be standing at the time. The curse to the program was that the moment the cock would see it, he would walk over very casually and sink his beak in it, thus destroying eggs that would sell from a dollar each up to five dollars an egg for the exotics.

When Father first learned of this, it nearly drove him wild and he fired off letters to neighboring zoos and the Game Department to see what could be done about it. The replies were more sympathetic than helpful. Some suggested that he distribute doorknobs or ping-pong balls around the cages. They'd found that occasionally a myopic cock would strike at one of these and give himself such a headache that he'd avoid taking a chance at anything round in the future. Others described a complicated procedure with cayenne pepper. This involved going into the cage and picking up one of the fresh eggs that had just been destroyed and taking it out to the zoo kitchen. Here the white and yellow inside would be drained out through the hole the cock had made, and the hollow shell repacked with cornmeal mixed with red pepper. Once you got the thing full, you sealed the hole with a piece of adhesive tape and then returned it to the cage, planting it tape side down. According to the reports, the cock was supposed to strike the egg and get his beakful of pepper and swear off forever.

Jim made a batch of these and casually distributed them through the pens and then everyone stood around to see what would happen. They got the whole range of reactions. Some of the birds seemed to recognize the eggs as second-hand and never hit them again—but promptly destroyed the first fresh ones laid. Others bit into them, looked astonished, and went wildly flapping around flipping their bills back and forth against the wire—and then promptly destroyed the next fresh ones laid. And a few bit in, looked astonished, and abandoned pecking for life.

The result was that little by little the zoo's own birds began to build up a "hatch"—with most of the eggs snatched by the keepers while they were still warm. These eggs were then accumulated in the zoo kitchen and set out, point down, in boxes of oatmeal. Twice a day Jim went through and methodically gave each egg a half turn, according to instructions from the Game Farm. It developed that the eight-hour shift was not necessary until incubation started, but a twelve-hour turn still was. So long as the eggs did not get either too cold or too warm, they would "keep" for several weeks before setting. "Keeping" in this case merely meant they would not be impaired for later hatching. It had no relation at all to the major problem with incubating eggs from birds in captivity: there was no way to tell whether the eggs were fertile until you'd set them. A hen would lay eggs day after day even if there was no cock in the cage at all. And even when the cock was available, unless he had fertilized this particular egg, it was completely worthless. This, of course, added another nice variable to the whole operation, so that all the agony of watching the cages, snatching the eggs, preserving them against shocks and chills, and then incubating them in an expensive piece of apparatus, could come to absolutely nothing. But it gave a pretty element of chance to the whole game.

When Father was convinced he had about all we could cope with, he suggested we drive out to Pratt (some sixty miles away) and pick up the Game Department's contribution. This proved to be a great delight. They had a fine operation going out there with row upon row of range cages, each one housing a cock, five or six hens, and a cornstalk shelter, and then in another part of the field there were dozens of white brooders up on legs so they stood waist-high, each made up of a little insulated, thermostatically controlled room, connected to a six- or eight-foot "run" so the chicks could grow and "harden" as they matured. There were no chicks hatched yet, so all I could do was make detailed drawings of the brooders in the expectation of building three or four myself while waiting for our eggs to hatch.

The Game Farm was also the fish hatchery for the southwest quadrant of the state, and we watched bass and perch by the thousands work their way in and out of long, watercressed ponds. The whole thing both depressed and cheered me. It all looked so businesslike and our approach was so naive and clumsy, but I was heartened with the thought that if they could do this with thousands of ordinary, wild pheasants, *surely* I could bring it off with a few hundred carefully tended exotic varieties.

The Game Farm pressed fifty bobwhite eggs on us, begging us to hatch what we could, and after keeping whatever we needed for the zoo (quail are too small to be good display stock or trade material) urged us to let the others go free. Their own incubators were rigged for the larger pheasant eggs, and they had too few bantams to set the bob-white eggs they'd accumulated. We sowed these in the oat-meal buckets along with everything else and headed home.

We decided to push the operation off the twenty-first of June, so I spent the evenings following the dog census getting the incubator tuned up. I started by filling the zinc tray from an aluminum teakettle I'd stolen from Mother upstairs, and was surprised to find that a tray only two inches deep and three feet long held eight teakettles of water! I got this filled and the hygrometer loaded with distilled water as instructed, latched the door, and dramatically threw the switch. The red light glowed and the incubator gave out a satisfying, businesslike hum. The thermometers behind the glass were vibrating quietly and the thing clearly was working.

Time after time I got down on my knees and weaved back and forth trying to pick up the streak of mercury, and ultimately—by using a hand flashlight—I could get it in only six or eight passes a look. The whole thing took on a slight ritual effect of the supplicant at the feet of The Great Brown Machine. It purred on and on, gradually warming the air and the water and the trays up to ninety . . . ninety-five . . . and the hundred-and-one-and-a-half the book required. At this point the thermostat apparently turned off the coils and the heat stabilized to the fraction of a degree. I was jubilant, as proud as if I'd done it myself.

But the humidity kept rising. The air inside kept getting wetter and wetter, beads of sweat began to appear on the instruments and the glass, and by the time it was completely saturated like a shower bath, I realized I was supposed to start fiddling with the little holes.

I slid back some of the lids and nothing happened. I pulled more of them and there seemed a slight diminution. I finally opened all of them all the way, and within an hour had dropped the humidity to the proper sixty-five percent. At this point I checked the thermometer again—to discover that it was fifteen degrees too low. If the thing had been filled with eggs, I would have wiped out the whole project. I'd brought in so much outside air through the holes that the heating unit couldn't keep up with it. Came then five days of hourly experimentation trying to hit a happy medium. The second day turned up a dramatic experience: the humidity began to fall like a desert and as the air got drier and drier, I was firmly shutting holes all over the place—without any kind of result. Ultimately, intelligence returned and I realized that the heat from the coils had "boiled" all the water out of the trays. Sure enough, they were bone dry with a rime of alkali left out of the Kansas water. This revealed the fact that not only were the eggs demanding turns on an eight-hour schedule, the water had to be replenished at the same time, or the thing would get so dry the shells would split. The margin of error seemed to be closing in on me.

By the weekend, however, I thought I'd solved all the subtleties that had evidenced themselves, and came the great morning for Setting The Incubator. During the trial-and-error sequence, Father had shown a distressing lack of interest in the mechanics of the thing, and except for a cheery, "Ah, you'll get it all worked out, Chuck!" in the midst of my threnodies, I could scarcely get his attention, much less drag him into the basement.

With the great egg move, however, he got caught up in it all again, and began delivering the stored eggs from the zoo—where he'd been keeping those received by mail and from the Game Farm, as well as those from the zoo itself. We laid the six trays out on the floor and began carefully to slide each egg into the appropriately sized wire holders. The peacock eggs seemed huge, even larger than chicken eggs, and we had to bend the largest racks open to accept them. The partridge and pheasant eggs were smaller, and they dropped in without distress, but the tiny quail eggs were so minute that we scarcely dared touch them. They were smaller than a thumb nail, and when they slipped in, point down, there was a breathless second between when you had to let them loose and when they "hit bottom" in the rack. So far as we could see, nothing cracked, and when everything was stowed, it made a very satisfying display: rows of pale blue peacocks, rows of tan and speckled pheasants—goldens, Lady Amhersts, silvers, mutants, Reeves, and ringnecks—the coarse brown eggs of the Chukar partridges, and the delicate bobwhites. With the exception of four empty rows, the thing had filled up nicely, and I was all for shoving the trays in and rolling ahead. Father couldn't bear to "waste all that space."

He ran upstairs and began calling around town. In a half hour he was downstairs again in triumph.

"Stauffer's Goat Farm says they've got some guinea eggs if we want 'em. Want to go along?"

"Don't you think we've got enough already?"

"No! Have you ever seen a guinea? Strange-looking thing. Skinny head. No tail. Its skin is all blue and Stauffer says it has perfectly black meat, but tastes like pheasant."

"Don't you think we'll have enough on our hands with the exotics?"

"Guineas are hardy. They won't be any trouble. I'll be right back."

He disappeared and I spent the hour checking the instruments, rereading the manual, and cautiously tilting the little racks back and forth to be sure everything would work. The book made it clear, once you got the thing going and incubation had started, there was no turning back. Ultimately, Father came in with a box full of blue eggs, each about the size of a pullet egg, and we distributed these in the remaining holes. Forty-eight holders, forty-eight guinea eggs.

I then lifted the trays—which were astonishingly heavy, each holding approximately a hundred eggs—and cautiously carried them to the machine. With Father's help I got them into the channels and slid them into the rack. Nothing dropped, nothing jammed or bound, and I shut the door with a feeling of impending doom. Throughout, the incubator had hummed and glowed, and within an hour had heated the eggs up to the proper hundred-and-one-and-a half degrees. And we were off. If everything held together, 21 days, 168 turnings, 80-odd gallons of water away, we'd know if anything was going to come of all this effort.

And so it began. I would rise every morning at 6:00 and dash down to the basement, fearing to find the red bulb out and the incubator cold. Much squinting at the instruments and reassurance that we'd safely passed the night. I'd then cautiously pull each tray two-thirds of the way out of the machine and tilt row upon row of the eggs. I was caught between my fear of breaking some by dumping them from side to side, and the threat of chilling them by having them in the bare air too long. Thus, working in a repressed hurry, I'd get all the eggs aimed in a different direction, shove the trays in solid, and shut the door. I'd then go to the laundry tubs and carefully get the water running at a hundred-and-one-and-a-half degrees testing with a photographic thermometer, load the teakettle, and make three trips to fill the zinc tray. By this time it would be nearly 7:00 and time for breakfast.

The day would progress, and with summer started, there were social things to do with friends as well as my carpentry—nailing the little brooders together and getting holding pens ready out behind the garage. The problem, of course, was that I didn't dare get too far away from home for fear of missing the 2:00 turning. This was a little difficult to explain to tennis partners and girls I'd offered to take to lunch, but the world is full of imperfections.

I'd drop off the young lady and make a mad dash for the basement. By 3:00 the shift would have been made—and the afternoon shot—so I got more wood work done than might have been expected. The situation was impossible, though, when it came to dating in the evening. You cannot imagine the glacial response you can get from a well-dressed girl when you tell her at 9:45 that either you're going to have to take her home or she'll have to wait while you turn and water an incubator. In two weeks, I'd wiped out every child I'd spent my senior year developing. By this time I was feeling tragically put upon. The inexorable 6:00 . . . 2:00 . . . 10:00 began to loom like water torture. I couldn't make a plan or initiate an effort without calculating ahead where it would leave me at two and ten.

But things were going on in the machine. According to the manual, "at ten days after the initiation of incubation, the eggs should be candled and any clear or cracked eggs eliminated to insure against later accidents and the release of hydrogen sulfide gases." I suspected this was a euphemism, but I was already thoroughly cowed and if the book feared accidents, even more then did I.

Candling involves holding an egg up to the light to see if there's anything going on inside. The booklet was nicely illustrated with a Japanese specialist in a white coat seated at a table in a dark room. He had a wooden box in front of him with a light in it and a hole slightly smaller than an egg cut in the top. He was putting eggs over the hole and the light shining through the shell was silhouetting the developing chick inside the egg. Simplicity itself. There were even three pictures of chicken eggs at seven, twelve, and seventeen days. The darkened blur in the center was obviously something and surely I could tell the difference between a "clear" egg (one that was infertile and therefore had no chick to develop) and one that would someday give us a bird.

I made a box and put a light bulb into it. I cut a hole about the size of a quarter in a piece of cardboard, nailed it over the bulb, and when the night was pitch black, turned out all the lights in the basement except for my candling box. The first thing I learned was that if you look through a holc in a darkened room at a bare 60-watt bulb, you are blinded for approximately forty-five seconds. This phenomena was substantiated roughly 200 times in the course of candling 600 eggs.

I further discovered that while the darkened shadow might be clearly seen in a white, thin-shelled chicken egg, it was almost impossible to determine in a blue, thick-shelled peacock egg, or a tan-brown Chukar, or a mottled pheasant; and a bobwhite egg was so small, that either you dropped it through the hole or your fingers blocked out anything there might be to see. Guinea eggs were absolutely opaque and they could have been filled with lead or lighter fluid so far as the candling box was concered.

This nonsense used up three nights with the whole family trying to guess whether or not there was anything in the things. The paler ones looked possible, but then again if we threw them out and they proved to have something in them we'd never forgive ourselves, so . . . after many hours of putting o's on probables and x's on possibles, we gave the whole thing up and decided to pray that there would be no accidents.

The third and final week arrived and, while I had destroyed my social life, I had three brooders ready to go which would hold a hundred chicks each, and I figured out a couple of emergency arrangements in case we should be unusually lucky. The book warned not to expect much above a fifty percent hatch, and as much as sixty percent would be most unusual. I was so mesmerized by my schedule by this time that I found myself reading ahead to see what I was supposed to feed the little things, actually beginning to delude myself that something might come of all this confusion after all.

On the morning of the nineteenth day, I rose at 6:00 and staggered down the stairs, throwing the light switch on as I opened the door and thinking to myself, the stupid light has blown out. There was enough light from the basement windows to navigate the steps, and I made it all the way to the bottom before it hit me. The red light on the incubator was out and the familiar hum was dead silent. The electricity was off in the whole house.

I dashed for the workbench, grabbed the flashlight, and slid up to the door on my knees. I finally located the mercury column and it stood at 78 degrees, 23 degrees "chilled." What to do? How long had it been off?

I raced back upstairs to check the electric clock in the kitchen. My hand-wound alarm clock had not been affected, but the electric over the sink was stopped at a little after 3:00. Three hours getting cold. Surely the heat of the eggs and metal and the water itself would have held some heat for a while. The full 23 degree drop couldn't have been so the whole time. But what to do now?

I bellowed for Father to get up and call the electric company, and I raced downstairs again. If I could think of something to introduce heat into the thing, we might be able to get it back up again. I thought of everything in the house that gave off warmth. Heating pad—required electricity. Kitchen range—electric again. Heat lamp—electricity. Hot water tank—gas! That would do it. I hurriedly grabbed a brace and bit off the tool wall and drilled a large hole through the side of the incubator about four inches from the bottom, hopefully hitting above all the insulation. The bit broke through clear, and I seemed to have found open space. I hastily closed all the little brass vents but one close by the door and in front of the egg trays themselves. I then filled the teakettle with pure hot water from the tap and began to pour it in through the hole in the top, not wanting to open the door and lose another degree. The hot water gushed in, hit the tray at the bottom with a splash, overflowed all over the inside floor, and began to run out my newly drilled hole. The procedure was functional. Now what would it do to the heat? I'd pour and look and pour and look, and fairly rapidly the heat inside began to rise. The fan, of course, was off, but the steam from the near-boiling water seemed to lift nicely, and I was hopeful that the heat registered at the midway where the thermometers were located would reflect the general state of affairs all over the inside. The hygrometer very quickly registered one hundred percent humidity, but this was the least of my worries at the moment.

It became a fatiguing but clear-cut routine. Fill the teakettle. Pour the water in. Kneel and squint at the thermometer. Struggle up and fill the teakettle. Round and round.

The rest of the family joined me to watch, and Father reported that the electric company knew the electricity was off and we weren't the only ones. Everything north of Thirteenth and west of Hillside was gone, too.

By the end of a half hour, I had the thing back up to a hundred-and-one and that mystical half degree and I was able to slow down the rhythm of the pouring. On what must have been about my fiftieth teakettleful, I was methodically pouring down the hole, standing in a half inch of water which stretched over the floor in every direction, when the electricity came on.

It entered the coils, which I was drenching from above, ran up the stream into the aluminum teakettle, and up my arm, straightening me out like a semaphore signal. My jaw snapped shut and the arm with the teakettle locked straight out at my side, still holding the handle, but mercifully directing the stream directly onto the floor instead of into the now fully charged machine. The red light came on. The fan started up. And I stood there signaling that the track was occupied, and no further trains should enter the block.

Much dashing around. Father pulled the incubator cord out of the wall—too late to do any good—and Mother screaming, "What's the matter? What's the matter?" When the singing in my ears began to subside, I tried moving my arms and found that everything seemed to be functioning although they evidenced considerable fatigue as if I might have been holding up a car while someone changed a tire or something.

By this time I'd noticed that Father had pulled the cord and this got through to me.

"No, put the plug back! That's what we've been waiting for!"

"But what about this water all over? Isn't it dangerous?"

I had to admit it just might be, so we hurriedly got two extension cords from upstairs and ran them from the incubator up the stairs, carefully plugging them into a first floor outlet. We could hear the fan below, humming peacefully again. I went back down to the bottom step and listened to the water seep slowly down the floor drains while the room filled with the smell of overheated rubber. When the light went out and the fan coasted to a stop, I realized that what I'd been smelling was the ordinary extension cord being unable to carry the heavy voltage of the heating coils. I yanked the cord out again, changed a fuse, and by dint of a long line of dry boards laid across the now only dampened floor, got the incubator properly running from its own outlet. This accounted for everything but the 6:00 egg turning, now long overdue, which would simply have to wait until the machine dried out. Fearful that I was creating a whole generation of lopsided birds, but being so scared of the supercharged machine itself, I quit fighting it and went up to breakfast. By 2:00 we were back on schedule, and I corked the hole I'd drilled and the immediate crisis was ended.

By now we were approaching the moment of truth. All the unknowns were adding up. Were the eggs fertile? Was the combination of heat and moisture close enough to have duplicated the wild state? Had the Great Blackout Crisis killed all of them off? Just some of them? But most important: we knew absolutely nothing about hatching anything. What all-important fact had we ignored simply because our one source of information assumed that "at least they would know enough to . . ."? The instruction book said that if the hatch was successful, we could expect our first pipping on the twenty-first day. This was supposed to be a see-able hole punched out by the chick to break the shell. According to the book, this effort would so exhaust the chick that nothing would happen for ten or twelve hours, and then the bird would start to serrate the top third of the shell until he'd pecked it off. He would then gather his strength and stagger out. This operation could take a whole additional day.

Came the morning of the twenty-first day. I turned each egg with extraordinary care, looking for some minute hole that would imply pipping. Nothing. Not one of all the 600 leaning eggs.

Same thing at 2:00. Still nothing. Not a one.

At 10:00 I dropped to my knees to check the thermometer before opening the door and there, standing on the tiny window sill and looking out at me through the glass, were two bright-eyed, brown little things each about the size of a nickel.

# 11

## *Of All Small Things*

I knelt on the concrete and stared back at the two little things, paralyzed. As I watched, a third dropped from the gloom above the little window, fell like a cork the length of the glass, and disappeared into the darkness below. They were coming out of the trays like popcorn! The truth had barely sunk in, when the two on the sill stepped back and dropped out of sight. The thought of what they must be falling into down there—water tray . . . heating coils . . . the hard, wooden floor—galvanized me into action and I staggered to my feet and jerked the cord out of the wall. This left me staring at the machine, trying to sort the situation out as little brown, fluff balls dropped past the thermometers at irregular intervals by ones and twos.

I could only conclude that something in there was hatching out dry and running the minute its feet touched the wire. I knew that so far as I'd been able to see, nothing had shown a sign of life at 2:00, so all of these things must have pipped, chipped off the end of their eggs, and hopped out in the past eight hours. The incubator book had promised us a day and a half at least—but the book had been written for chickens. *Something* in there had an accelerated timetable.

Never having seen any of our kinds of birds as chicks, the only idea I had of what they should look like was by reasoning from analogy. I'd seen baby chicks at Easter and they looked so big. A grown pheasant or guinea or peacock was bigger than a chicken, so their chicks should be larger than a chicken chick. These little brown things were much smaller. Zipping past the window, they seemed about as big as my thumbnail, so they must be the bobwhites. But what to do about them? I was back at the cold incubator dilemma again.

If I opened the door and pulled all the trays out to collect the tiny things, I'd run the chance of chilling the new ones hatching out, but if I didn't do something, I was going to drown, or worse, what we had. Weighing this-and-thats furiously, I finally grabbed the screened tray covers that had been under the bench for nearly a month now, flung myself on my knees, and started in.

I opened the door cautiously and heard a chorus of tiny peeps within the now stilled machine, and every so often another would flash past on its way down. I figured I'd best try to retain whatever was still in the trays and then hope to recover something of what had fallen by. Cautiously I pulled the top tray forward, and I got the full picture in a look.

Here was this tray with the same row upon row of eggs I'd been turning so carefully for nearly a month now, and all the big ones looked just the same—with one difference. Every so often one of them had a hole in it the size of a match stick. Poking out through each of these little holes was a tiny bill. Some of them were bright yellow and some were sort of coffee-colored with several varieties of tan. Some of the little beaks were motionless as if the puncturing process had exhausted them, while some were pecking in and out—but in every case, with the larger eggs, there was just one hole.

Not so with the rows of the tiny, white quail eggs. They looked like a grenade had gone off. A third of them were completely empty with a neat little lid chipped off of each one and dropped down between the wire holders. Another third had their lids off and the little beady-eyed chicks were thrashing their way out, still damp but furiously active, while the products of the empty eggs were running up and down the trays like crazy. They were the little fluffs I'd seen and they were scuttling around so fast you could scarcely follow them. Some were running back and forth crosswise between the pews. Others were going up and down and over the long way, and they were mixed up with the large eggs and collecting in the corners and peeping away with microscopic chirps so the place was seething. I whipped up a tray cover and let it down carefully over the edges till it had safely "boxed" the tray in, though I could still see through the wire mesh of the lid. The activity was still wild, but at least they were no longer vaulting over the sides. I looked down the drawer runners and they looked clear, so I slid the first tray back in place.

The same procedure worked on the rest. Each tray had had three or four rows of quail eggs in it, so they were all developing chicks at a similar rate, and every layer was equally lively. Several times I had to brush one of them back just as he started over the lip, but I managed to catch them all in time, and fairly quickly got each tray screened and shoved back in position. This brought me to the point of going after the ones that had fallen out, and I found I shrank from seeing what had happened to them. I closed the door to keep the heat in and tried to think where to go from there.

Clearly the chicks could not have fallen over the sides of the trays since these were held by the racks' runners. The ones I'd seen would have had to drop from the front ends, and I knew there was a similar place for air circulation in the back. The ones in front had probably fallen all the way to the bottom of the machine, but the ones behind had presumably dropped into the water trays and if so would have been drowned by now. I'd never bothered to see if the heating coils were covered by the water tray. If not, and they were exposed . . .

Both because I thought if they were still alive but wet they'd have to be dried out, and because I didn't have the nerve to face any drowned or burned chicks, I temporized by running upstairs and getting a large bath towel off the rod over the tub. I forced myself to go back down the stairs and found myself wasting time looking for a cardboard box to hold whatever I'd find. Once I became aware of this delaying action, I located a carton with old toys in it, dumped them on the floor, and lined the bottom with the towel. I then brought the box over to the incubator and knelt to collect what had fallen.

I opened the door, almost nauseated with distaste, and with squinted eyes pulled the heavy, zinc water tray out from under the egg trays. It barely cleared the base of the door as it came into the light, and I realized that it hadn't been cleaned for four weeks since I'd been filling it from the front by merely pouring new water over the edge. Somewhat to my relief, I found that what had looked dark and wet inside was now revealed as being a rather sludgy mess, but at the end of its eight-hour stint only about a quarter of an inch deep with water—instead of the two inches it would have been had I refilled it according to the next schedule.

And sure enough, slithering around in the slime were fifteen or twenty little bugs, their fluff stuck to them, but their eyes as bright as ever, and seemingly as lively as their brethren above. I pulled the tray halfway out of the incubator, and then expected the little things to hold still out of gratitude for being rescued. They shot around like so many water beetles, not the least interested in being caught. Little by little I got them, a churning chick at a time, and carefully set them down in my toweled box. In my hand—and still thrashing around—they felt like a very lively acorn, and so far as I could see, were not the least the worse for the wear. As soon as I'd dropped the last one into the box and let him scuttle over the towel long enough to dry off his underside, I picked them up a handful at a time and redistributed them among the six egg trays back in the incubator. I was so fearful of some of the new ones getting out that I'd slide the cover back just the width of a chick. This gave the effect of sort of mailing them into the slots, but I managed it without losing anybody, and was finally beginning to think that there was hope.

Thus fortified, I got the flashlight and peered into the bowels of the machine to see what was on the floor. The heavy, black heating rods were fully exposed now, but the water tray had covered them, and there were no chicks caught there. On the wooden floor—which was nearly three feet below the top egg tray—there was another dozen of the little things. Two up near the front had been killed by the fall, and another failed to survive later, but aside from these tiny tragedies, the remainder were even livelier than the rest since they'd had a full, smooth floor to limber up on. It took me twice as long to corral these without hurting them, but in another fifteen minutes I had them replaced in the trays above, the casualties removed, and the water tray filled and back in place. I slammed the door shut and shoved in the plug, trusting again that the operation had not suffered too much chilling. The whole struggle had taken less than an hour, but with the door open so much of the time, the incubator had cooled quickly. I left it heating up again, and there seeming no more to be done there I got to my feet, took the flashlight, and went out into the side yard. In the darkness I could see the long, white brooder houses, and I switched on the heating element in each so it could prepare for the coming guests. Each house had a white bulb inside to light the warming room, and a red bulb on the outside to show the heaters were working. With these glowing efficiently, I gave up and went to bed. Mother and Father were at a Little Theater play at Linwood Park, and I was too tired to wait up to report the latest events.

The next morning started the great mess of coping, and for the following six weeks, I doubt if I've ever worked so hard in my life, before or since. The routine developed thus: hour after hour, more and more of the chicks "came off," and it soon became a game of figuring out which ones were ready to be transferred to the brooders. According to the book, once the chick had hatched and was out of the shell, he could stay in the trays for a day at least. He was still carrying enough of the yolk from the egg that he was neither hungry nor needed food, but he did need the warmth of the incubator to dry out and build up his strength. At the same time, you couldn't leave them in the trays too long for fear of their trampling each other and smothering somebody. Still the popcorn problem. It was like trying to decide when to lift the popper off the heat. You don't want to leave it so long it scorches, but if you take it off too early, you waste half the kernels. Decisions, decisions.

Every hour I'd pull out a tray and peer in trying to decide which ones were ready to move. The quail choice was easy. They exploded, dried, and flashed around so quickly that by the end of the first day, I'd scooped out handfuls into my towel-box and rushed them to the brooders in the yard. By supper everyone that was going to appear, had, and been moved on.

The chicks in the larger eggs gradually pipped, and then, very slowly, chipped off the end of their shells. Some took a full twenty-four hours to work the cap off, and then would just lie there, all knotted together, without trying to get out of the shell for another half a day. Once out in the air, they took further hours to dry. The sluggish advance of this operation was as nerve-racking as the explosion of the quail. Several of the pheasants removed the ends of the eggs, but refused (or were unable) to get out, and after agonizing with them for many hours, I finally helped them into the world. Ultimately every one of these died or were so crippled they had to be killed.

I found the whole hatching process unpleasant, and I was rather repelled by it all, but once everybody was out, dry, and fluffy, things became quite delightful. Almost at once I lost track of what kinds of chicks had come out of which eggs. Some were speckled like baby fauns, others were leaf-colored, and some were golden like Easter ads. The little guineas looked like everything else when they were running around, but if you picked them up and ruffled their fluff "against the grain," you could see the astonishing blue skin beneath.

One of the great delights was the way that everything was cheeping and scratching and dashing around as if there were all sorts of things that had to be done and very little time to do them in. Great running about and excitement. I began to distribute the pheasants-partridges-peacocks into the two remaining brooders, and dropped the guineas into one of the emergency brooders I'd laid out on the floor. The latter was primitive, but the birds were supposed to be hardy—and my main attention was on the exotics. From the moment they were dry, they were worth several dollars apiece, and if I could bring them to adulthood, the whole operation represented hundreds of dollars'-worth of trade in new animals for the zoo.

The exhausting aspect of the thing was the feeding. All the game birds had to have food in front of them all the time. This meant, literally, an endless stream of stuff sixteen hours a day. The idea of the sport was to find substitutes for the kinds of food the chicks would have been eating with their parents in the field. Since they lived on live worms and bugs and grubs and things, they went in big for protein at first, mixed with some greenery, and as they grew up, the ratio of meat-substitute to leafy foods gradually shifted to seed and grain over a period of three months. What this meant to me was an unending stream of hard-boiled eggs and head lettuce, mixed with turkey mash, and eventually cracked chicken feed.

The odor of boiled eggs still comes to me on hot, windless nights, and strangles the back of the throat. It seemed to me I was living in a world of cold, clammy whites, and sulfurous yellows. During the first weeks of July, I would put three or four dozen store eggs to boil every evening, and after they'd banged around in the water for twenty minutes, with one or two inevitably splitting open, I'd carry them in their pans to the back porch to cool. Come morning, I'd sit down and laboriously peel off the shell and then for what seemed like hours, push the contents through frames of window-screen wire. For the first few days, I sieved only the yellow and threw the white away, but as the chicks grew, I was instructed to add more and more white until eventually the whole thing was going through the screen with the little squiggles collecting on the pans below. If someone had earlier suggested that the major qualifications for successful game bird culture were a strong thumb and a bad cold, I would not have understood. By the time I had shelled and hand-pressed over a thousand hard-boiled eggs in the first month, the sight and aroma of a picnic would flatten me from a block away. At this time in the Thirties, eggs were extraordinarily cheap, but to keep the cost even lower, I purchased cold storage eggs which had failed to sell, and were therefore of questionable use. The fumes that fifty eggs pressed on a hot Kansas day . . . just the thought of it makes the eyes water!

The . . . ugh, eggs . . . were mixed with chopped lettuce. Had I been a pheasant hen, I would have pecked grass and weeds into tiny chips and dropped these in front of the chicks. This being inappropriate, I substituted by shearing up two heads of lettuce into minute shreds each day and mixing these with the—other stuff. By the end of the month, it was requiring four or five heads a day, but lettuce at least is odorless. All of this, mixed with an increasing dust of turkey mash and some finely ground oyster shells, provided the meals. And they ate constantly, of course, interrupting only occasionally for a short nap. I don't know what else I was expecting, having provided them with limited recreational facilities, but this endless consumption of food struck me as being in poor taste. Subsistence is one thing, but this verged on gluttony. After a week or so, the book said to introduce water jugs into the brooders, so filling upside-down Mason jars was added to the routine. This shelling, sieving, chopping, mixing, filling, shelling, sieving, chopping, et cetera, went on and on from sunrise to sunset.

Had I known, the eating habits of the diverse varieties would have given me an index to what was going to come of all this effort. Their table manners registered a correlation that would have sent a psychologist running to the foundations for publishing money. The quail approached the food trays with purpose, stood on either side in orderly rows, and their little heads pecked up and down like Swedish toys. The partridges, somewhat larger, but equally purposeful, ate and drank with some intelligence. Not so the pheasants. A more stupid, disorganized collection of creatures I had never met. They stood in the food trays and waded in the water. A dozen would keep fifty from eating, and then a hundred would rush on top of each other, smothering those on the bottom. Some never learned to eat and gradually starved to death, while others never left the trays and were progressively trampled.

The mortality of the things stunned me. Each morning when I slid back the brooder covers there would be a half dozen flattened out like cardboard. Bodies would have drowned in the water holders and hung themselves on wires or protruding strips of insulation. I tried increasing the number of food trays and found they were now falling asleep in the mixture and suffocating. I tried dividing them into small groups and they killed themselves off just as remorselessly as in the mass. I covered the water trays with wire so they had to poke their beaks through to get to liquid—and another dozen died of thirst while ten went to sleep with their heads through the screen and drowned.

The old saying about not having the sense to come in out of the rain was created for them. After the first few weeks, I opened a door in the front of each brooder so the chicks could run out in screened runways and get sun and exercise. When they weren't baking at two o'clock, too stupid to go back in the shade, they were soaked by a sudden thunderstorm, too stupid to get out of the damp.

We had started with roughly 50 quail and 50 peacock eggs and we had had astonishing fertility in these, producing about 35 chicks each. They thrived in the best of health. We had begun with 450 pheasant eggs of which something less than 300 hatched, and these were wiping themselves out with both hands. The more they died, the more they irritated me. While I had been crushed at losing the first three bobwhites, every time one of the pheasants expired (their favorite stunt was to go to sleep with their heads in corners and smother in the crack; I tried rounding the corners with cardboard until they pecked holes in it, stuck their heads through, and strangled) I would take it as a personal insult and be driven back to mashing eggs in a fury.

However, by the end of the first month, apparently all the suicidal types had made away with themselves, and by August I was able to lean back and enjoy what was left. They began to feather very quickly, and the cocks of each variety were developing tiny tails and headcrests. The bobwhites got plumper and plumper and enormously tame. When I'd approach their brooder they would scuttle over to me and perch in my hand or on my arm. They slept in such an astonishing manner that half of their sleep was shot just by my showing them off to visitors. When it began to get dusk, they would make a perfect cirle with all their tails pointing to the center, and all their heads out. They would then go to sleep, nicely packed side by side so they looked like a beautiful, brown wreath. Our hunting friends assured us that this is the way they sleep in the field, and if a dog or coyote finds them, they explode in every direction so the animal is completely confused by the clutter.

By mid-August, I had most of the quail and partridge in beautiful condition, absolutely every one of the guineas (we hatched 48 and we slaughtered 48 for the freezer a year later), and something less than 200 pheasants and peafowl. What there were were fortuitously distributed through the various types, so we were going to have many pairs of everything to show for the effort. About this time the pheasants started fighting among themselves, so I shot another week clipping the ends off their beaks, but it was clear that by Labor Day the holding pens would be full and Father could start dickering for trades again.

It was right along here that I was so emboldened with my skill at raising things I decided to have a go at waterfowl, too. On the strength of my vast experience in game bird incubation, I wrote off to the Fish and Game Hatchery for data on wild ducks, geese, and swans: mallards and teal, Canadian, and mute, to be precise. Back came the word and pamphlets, and sure enough, with the usual perversity of the pesky things, absolutely everything I'd learned in the pheasant and quail business was done exactly in reverse for the paddling types. Once again it hung on making the egg feel at home. A pheasant might have put her nest on the damp ground, but this was purely relative. Dampness in an upland field was nothing compared to the life span of a duck egg laid in a marsh and sat upon by a dripping mother just back from a short cruise. The result was that the hatchery brains urged the abandonment of an electric incubator, and the use of plain, old, clucking setting hens to do the work. They suggested that a nest be built of clay in a box, and when the hen sat on the eggs, the clay should be kept moist and the hen lifted at regular intervals to spray the eggs with water. This sounded like a fast way to give a hen a head cold, but I'd come on so many unlikely things in the past six weeks that I no longer challenged anything.

I made me three setting coops out beside the garage and then wrote back to the Game Department to ask about a source of eggs. The whole idea seemed to amuse them (I suspected that no one had ever really tried the routines in their pamphlets—they were just theoretically possible!) so they replied to say they were spreading the word among the game wardens and would try to find me three clutches of eggs from wild nests.

This challenged me, and I made the rounds of the local feed stores to see if any of them could get me three setting hens from their customers. Ross McCausland's down by the MoPac tracks soon called to say that he'd located some on a farm south of town if I was willing to pay three or four dollars apiece. This sounded like a colossal bargain compared with the sheaf of money I'd put out for the machine, so I got Father to drive me out and I met my first setting hen. Had I had anything to do with a farm in my formative years, I'd have known what a setting hen was, but I was surprised to find it to be an oversized variety of ordinary chicken which apparently in certain seasons feels an overwhelming urge to hatch something. It starts shuffling around the barnyard all fluffed out and clucking endlessly, presumably in practice for keeping track of a dozen chicks. Back in the old days when farmers let hens raise their own progeny, the owner would have let the hen collect twelve or fifteen eggs in her nest, and then she'd go to "sitting on them"—keeping them warm and covered, continuously, for the required twenty-one days. Nowdays, when all hatching is done by hatcheries, the farmer either breaks up the nest and locks the hen outside of the coop until she gets over the idea, or converts her to frozen baker for the Thanksgiving trade.

I brought mine home with me and kept them in the mood by filling three nests with ping-pong balls while waiting for the eggs to arrive. These came in shortly, mailed from three separate wildlife installations in western Kansas, not too far from Colorado. I later learned that while the wardens had assembled the geese and swan eggs from wing-shot captives, the mallard and teal were actually stolen in the field. The wardens had made the rounds of the various nesting grounds and deliberately raided nests they knew about. When they found ones with only one or two eggs in them, they lifted them on the presumption that it was the beginning of a clutch and the ducks hadn't settled down to serious incubating yet. A duck will lay up to a dozen eggs before she feels like she's got a full house and starts to set. By their taking only one or two, the hen just lays that many more to get back to her basic dozen. This way nobody gets hurt, and the world ends up with a duck or two per nest more. The eggs arrived in the perennial oatmeal, packed in empty tomato juice cans and mailed like cookies to Junior at camp.

By the time they came, I'd gained a firm respect for the anger of a setting hen. On a couple of occasions I had tried to lift one of them up to show off the splendid display of ping-pong balls beneath, and each time they'd slammed their beaks into me with such purpose that they'd thinned the humor of the situation and I'd abandoned the joke. This was going to be a real problem once the setting began, because each hen had to be lifted four times a day and the eggs and nest wet down through the full 28 days it takes to hatch a duck. I finally worked up a combination of fur-lined leather gloves and an old school jacket with towels safety-pinned around the right forearm. Thus armored, I'd plunge in, scooping the hen up in the right hand and shaking water around with the left. Half a clean vinegar bottleful per soaking seemed to meet all the requirements. If the hens objected to the sodden undercoating, they never mentioned it, and they proceeded through the long month in splendid health.

When the three wet nests began to hatch, I'd transferred the responsibility to the hens, so I could watch the pipping and hatching in fine detachment, and I was pleased to find the mothers just as capable as I was. Within a couple of days, all three were off the nests with little rows of ducklings-goslings-cygnets scuttling along behind them like the cover of a Caldecott winner.

The hens ate cracked corn and chicken feed, while the youngsters ate turkey mash and pellets swimming in a damp, soup-like arrangement. I'd feared that this difference was going to be a problem, but by sprinkling some of the feed on the mash, everybody got eating out of the same dish in no time, and within a few days I could feed the hens on the ground, and the little ones slurped from the bowls. I found quite a corollary between the intelligence of the upland birds and the web-footed types. The Canadian geese were almost as stupid as the pheasants had been, but with a hen brighter than I was, we eliminated the mortality. The goslings, though, while beautiful to watch, were too dumb to find their way back to the nest if one got separated by a large leaf or high stick. I spent hours rescuing somebodies, honking in a tiny racket only three feet from home. As they grew up, they were also difficult to manage, because they were too obtuse to drive.

Something with some intelligence can be driven toward a coop or recaptured from a hole in a fence by flapping your arms at them and as they retreat you can get them headed in the right direction. The goslings were too dumb to react to anyone flapping or trying to grab them and would either run right into you or sheer off between your legs and defeat the whole idea.

The swans were only slightly smarter, and it seemed to me they were already showing the mean streak that swans are noted for. Adult swans have a well-established reputation for being the foulest-tempered birds loose and the generally contentious note seemed to appear early in the cygnets.

But the ducks were a total delight. They were bright-eyed and cheerful, eminently intelligent, and very affectionate. They'd patter around the lawn behind their foster mother, enormously curious, testing this and turning that over. They were soft and plump and seemed to enjoy being picked up, whereupon they'd nestle down in the palm of your hand and make satisfied, purring-like quacks. I'd find a nice patch of green turf and sit down on it and they'd come streaming across the grass and hop up in my lap with such flattering pleasure at my having come to visit them that I wasted half the time I should have been giving to the growing pheasants and peafowl. All of the waterfowl lived and thrived, and I demanded a parent's claim on their future. I told Father he could use the geese and swans for trading material, but I wanted all my ducks transferred to our own zoo and released in the ponds unclipped. He let me get away with this, and they made a splendid collection in the fall—the young teal drakes with their beautiful turquoise wing feathers, and the fat, red fronts of the mallards showing real style.

All of "my" ducks spent the winter there, even though you could see them standing very quietly with an eye cocked to the sky when the autumn migrations flew overhead, headed south. They spent the following spring and summer with us, too, but on their second autumn, probably a third of them joined the long V's above and left, and by the following year they had all flown away. I was delighted, and of all the odd things the two "zoo summers" got me involved in, nothing gave me as much satisfaction as the ducks and the quail.

Labor Day arrived, and I faced up to school again, with something attempted, something done. In the last weeks before enrollment, I methodically transferred stock from one place to another, getting myself divested of wildlife so I could concentrate on being a freshman. Everything was fully feathered out and looking like whatever it was supposed to be. I returned the setting hens to the farmer and moved all the waterfowl to the zoo. The geese and swans were wing-clipped, and Father lifted them out in pairs during the winter's trades. I took my beloved quail with me when I gave the hens back and in return for the paid-up hens I got the farmer to stack some shocks of kaffir corn and wheat and barley along the fences in his bottom woodland. I then turned the quail loose, lifting them out of the crates one at a time. Like the ducks, they loved to nestle down in my hands and rub their cheek feathers against my fingers. As I'd hold them up, almost none of them flew away, even though it was the first time they'd been handled without screens on every side, and I had to set them down in the weeds along the fence-row. Once on the ground, they sort of explored where I was standing, and soon began to scuttle across my shoes and between my feet. By the time I had all of them lifted out, they were beginning to spread farther afield, and within half an hour they had all disappeared among the cornstalks or along the creek-side underbrush. I feared at the time that my affection for them may have signed their death warrant. If they assumed they could trust all humans, they would be wiped out before winter. My only hope was that their natural instincts would override their initial experience, and if they could survive their first shotgun blast, they would know their lives as they had to be lived.

From the zoo's point of view, my three dozen peafowl were the major success. I even had more cocks than hens, which was more than I had any right to expect, and they were building toward some magnificent plumage. Two-thirds were the usual metallic blues, but ten were pure white. I found these unnatural and bleached looking, but Father was particularly excited about the whites, and to my surprise most of the visitors were more impressed with them than all the subtle coloring of the regular ones. The neighbors were unusually kind in their acceptance of my side-yard bird farm, and when I got on campus, I found I'd met half my profs at one time or another as someone who had come or was brought over on some Sunday afternoon to see the collection. Father had respectable holding pens built at the zoo and we moved the peafowl out and over there to hold and display while he dipped into them for his trading. Being able to throw in a pair or two of peacocks ultimately swung more deals than the bears and hoofed stock he was working with, and the peafowl repaid the cost of the incubator all by themselves.

The pheasants were useful but in a small change sort of way, and we left them in the pens across the back lot through the fall and winter, until Father had thinned them a little at a time. A new helper at the zoo came out and cared for them, releasing me first for studies and then later so I could serve as a grader, et al, in the History Department. Right up to the day Father traded off the last pair, however, the pheasants gave me a hard time. They were kept in long chicken-wire pens, which had high boards around the base and wire overhead about five feet high. No matter how long we had the nervous things, they never got used to anyone, and the approach of the feeder or a cat or an airplane or the shadow of a leaf waving in the wind would send them straight up in the air en masse.

If you like that sort of thing, it was a pretty spectacular display. Someone would walk around the corner of the house and 200 red, blue, brown, gold, and silver birds would roar right to the tops of the pens. There would be a great racket, much beating of wings and wire banging around, and two or three would tear through a hole and be loose. Mother would rush to the phone to call me at the History Department and say, "There's a pair of ringnecks and a golden over at the Fletchers'." My fat friend and fellow grader, Kelley Sowards, would join me and we would trot the three blocks home to get the nets. We had two corded fishnets about three feet across with six-foot handles and off we'd go in the neighborhood.

We found the pheasants were terribly fast on the ground, of course, and there were really only two ways of catching the things. One was to drive them into some kind of a corner—which sufficiently baffled them that you could slam a net down over them—or you could net them out of the air. The latter was great sport, and oddly enough, the most effective way of doing it most of the time. If a pheasant has something to run along, like the side of a house or a hedge, he'll go indefinitely. If he's out in the open, however, he'll usually stop and flatten down into the grass, presumably to keep from being seen. He'll then watch whatever is after him until he's sure he's discovered and then at the last possible second, flush straight into the air.

Sowards and I got highly skilled with this technique, and one of us would circle around behind him, while the other would hold his attention by moving very slowly forward. When the rear man was in position, the two of us would start toward him with nets shoved out in front of us about a foot above the ground like mine detectors. The sight of my 200-pound friend (who is now Dean of a university) tiptoeing across the turf like Les Sylphides was almost too much to bear, but if I could keep from collapsing, we would converge at the bird. At the last step it would flush straight up, and then the rear man would make a sweep out of the air and net him. We'd fold him in the net, and while I was repairing the break with the five hundredth piece of baling wire, Sowards would throw the bird back in the pen. I suspect we re-collected fifty or sixty like this over the fall and winter, and only lost a half dozen the whole time.

Father was trading them off steadily, but the pens were getting more and more banged around, and the police dog at the girls' gym instructor's house got an unending delight out of sending the birds into the air. By the time Father had bartered away the last of them, I had had pheasants up to the epiglottis.

The incubator, ultimately, had paid for itself several

times over, and by dint of trading upwards with the stock, the summer produced over a thousand dollars' worth of furred animals for Riverside. Having gotten the feel of the egg in all its most subtle ramifications, it might be thought that I'd found a career here for profit if not for fun, but—supreme irony—I never raised another bird, and as things broke, the incubator was sold the next summer, having produced its one single hatch and then oblivion.

# 12

# *Fearful Symmetry*

Back at the zoo fall had come with coeds in wool skirts, the smell of football in the air, and for the parks an odd mixture of wild success and a genuine disaster.

The zoo itself was flourishing. The city had taken it to its bosom to exceed anything Father could wish for, and his trades were spinning like gears, belts, and flywheels. When he'd started, he'd had to trade three for one, then two for one, and then one to one as his stock grew more respectable. The end result was just as he'd predicted, but the side effect was the surprise. He'd been meeting so many zoo directors all over the place, and corresponding with so many keepers across the Mississippi Valley, that before he knew it he'd become the unpaid broker for the Midwest animal trading business. When a zoo would lose an animal the word would go out, "Get in touch with Bernie and see if he knows anybody with an extra thus-and-such." Conversely, when somebody got something they had no room for, they'd leave word with Father as the logical clearing-house. Father got an enormous delight out of this, and the more complicated he could get things, the more pleased he was.

"Mae, I brought off a wild one today! Tulsa's been trying to get a camel to make a pair and I've finally got it worked out. Tulsa'll give an extra zebra to Cheyenne. Cox at Cheyenne's going to give K.C. two bobcats, and Swope Park'll ship Tulsa a camel in exchange. Neat, huh? Everybody's satisfied. Tulsa's a bit long, and Kansas City's a bit short, but K.C. was long on the leopard thing I worked with Dallas, so they're about even again."

"Did you get anything out of it, Bernie?"

"No, not now, at least. But Tulsa knows they're a shade up and maybe they'll be more sympathetic when I go after one of their buffalo this summer."

The trades were only the beginning, though. Most of his acquisitions had come in the early spring or summer, so by fall we suddenly had "little things" appearing in every pen. The newspapers were carried away, and between new animals—mostly hay-eaters, the smaller cats, the prairie hunters, and babies of every size and shape—they had copy for weeks on end without repeating themselves once.

This steady increment swelled the crowds, lined every curving walk with pens, and accomplished exactly what MacDonald had warned Father about. The food bill was rising inexorably, and the need for extra keepers was even worse. After much martyrdom on both sides, MacDonald had gone to the Park Board for the first and then the second helper for Jim and Saylor. MacDonald had brought the Board around by showing them how a certain portion of the two new salaries could come from WPA funds, but everyone knew these might disappear overnight and the city would be stuck with the full price.

The new help precipitated the tragedy. They revealed in a frightening manner how skilled Jim and Saylor had been without their sophistication really showing. The new men were assigned as understudies to the old hands and the latter's apparent nonchalance with the animals led them astray. The crisis developed in the bear cages.

Our bear pits were a massive, Alcatraz-like arrangement that proved if iron bars do ever a prison make, this was it. We had bars to shatter the mind of man. The pits began with a great, poured-concrete mountain in the center which held eight bear dens. Growing out from the mountain in pie-shaped wedges were the open cages, defined by thick, ugly iron rods which rose ten feet in the air and then hooked down toward the poor bears as if they were begging to claw something that tried to escape. These walls of bars marching down off the cement mountain were bad enough, but every two cages were separated by a barred corridor or alley which gave the keepers access to the dens in the center. These alleys added their own bars and points, so no matter where you stood you were staring through a forest of rusty, black iron. The prison effect was reinforced by a great collection of gratings and doors with heavy drop locks across them—all of which might have had some reason if we'd been housing grizzlies or polar bears, but which looked ridiculous with our stock.

We still had nothing in the bear department but the little black specimens that you see in Yellowstone or the Smokies. These shuffled around in a harmless way and the largest scarcely came up to the waist of a grown man. I'd always been impressed myself with how peaceful the collection was, and with the fantastic fertility we had going. Every cage had one or two cubs in it all the time, and the place fairly sloshed with togetherness and the family scene.

The cubs always began as fat, round little things, and then very quickly got long and clumsy in their first year of adolescence, and then, if we hadn't managed to get them traded off beforehand, ended up as rangy parents themselves. Everybody looked good except for one pitiful specimen with three legs. The public thought he'd been injured in a fight and ought to be destroyed. The fact was that he'd been born with three legs and was perfectly happy with his tripodal lot and by now was the proud father of some fifteen healthy cubs through the years. Since he was so identifiable, he got special attention from the keepers and, being untradeable, had probably been on the mountain as long as any bear in the place.

One of the new men, after watching Jim clean and feed the island for a couple of weeks, had been given the full responsibility for the bear pits. This meant chopping up sixty or seventy pounds of horsemeat each morning, lacing in some unsold supermarket fish, and heaving the mixture into steel baskets to be carted over to the cages. Once there, he was supposed to unlock the door to an access alley, take in the proper amount of food, lock the outside alley door, walk down the alley to the cage door, throw the meat under the feeding grating, then, while they ate, drop the iron door to the den, open the barred door to the den, lock it behind him, and go inside and scrub it down. He was then supposed to do everything in reverse, locking and unlocking things till he had the bears inside the den and the outside area scrubbed down. Needless to say, this took a couple of hours to get all the way around the island, and was powerfully tedious, but Jim had been doing it for years and nobody thought a thing about it.

About the second week of the new man's responsibility, a woman came screaming into the Lion House shrieking, "Help! Somebody, help! A bear's eating a man out there."

Bob Saylor heard the uproar from the zoo kitchen and ran out into the public room to see what was the matter. The woman, who had run nearly a block to report this, was gasping, out of breath, and near hysteria. Saylor heard her only once, yelled at a man and his son who were standing in front of the lion cages, "Get the keeper in the Bird House and send him to the bear pits!" and dashed out the door, sprinting for the prison block himself.

As he approached it, he could see half a dozen people yelling in front of a cage with the adults screaming and throwing things through the bars, and kids crying and hiding their eyes. Inside the keeper was down on his back, a mass of blood, with a bear on top of him hanging on to his arm while the man kicked and thrashed underneath. The three-legged bear was standing on a ledge above, watching the whole thing passively, and two small cubs were huddled against the far bars, apparently terrified.

Saylor dashed in and found to his mixed horror and relief that every one of the doors was unlocked, and the inner alley door was standing half open. He picked up the steel basket in one hand and a scoop shovel which was lying there in the other and dashed into the cage. He slammed the side of the basket down on the bear's head as hard as he could, dropped it, and began flailing away with the flat of the shovel. The bear hung on for a few seconds longer and then cringed and began to back away. Saylor kept hitting it in the face and nose to keep it off balance and keep it from charging him until it finally spun around and slunk off into the den.

Saylor hastily checked to see if the other animals were holding their ground and then turned his back on them and dropped to the keeper who was down. At the same time, a citizen who had been yelling and trying to divert the bear from outside ran down the corridor between the cages and came in to help. The two of them slid the keeper out into the alleyway and Saylor slammed the cage door behind him with his foot just as Jim came running up.

Saylor shouted, "We're all right! Get an ambulance!" while he tore off his own shirt and undershirt to wrap the wounds and slow the bleeding. The keeper was conscious but terrified, and his leg, thigh, and forearm were badly mangled. The torn flesh was hideous to look at, but it was impossible to tell how seriously he was hurt. The ambulance arrived very shortly and Bob and the new keeper were taken to the hospital.

When Jim had phoned for the ambulance, he had also called Father at the City Building and then run back to help Saylor. Once the two had left for the hospital, Jim had asked the witnesses if they would stay long enough to tell his supervisor what had happened. Those who had actually been there when the attack occurred all agreed to wait and Father roared up in a few minutes.

Jim sketched out what he knew and Father dispatched him to the Lion House to notify Mr. MacDonald and to call the hospital to see if there was anything he could do there. He then began to question the witnesses and finally got the story. It was disgustingly simple. The keeper had obviously thought all this locking and unlocking was unnecessary with such harmless animals as these little black bears and had simply skipped all the routine and thought, if he thought at all, that he'd just do everything at once. He had therefore casually unlocked all the doors and strolled into the cage carrying the meat. He'd thrown the meat down, turned around, tossed the basket back in the alley, and as he turned back into the pit the mother had shot across the enclosure and seized him by the leg. There seemed no earthly reason for the attack. The cubs were peacefully playing completely across the cage from the keeper, the three-legged father was sleeping on an upper level, and the keeper had made no abrupt or threatening moves. If there was any accounting for it, it would have to have been the change from the routine she had always known and she may have assumed that this difference implied some kind of invasion of her family space.

In any event, she had seized him by the lower leg, and as he fell she lunged at his thigh. He tried to beat at her eyes with his fist and she seized his forearm and the agony had been at this stage when Saylor had arrived. Father thanked everyone, got their names, and by this time Peterson had arrived and Father went with him in the patrol car to the hospital. The keeper had been badly chewed, but the injury was limited to the muscles with little bone or nerve involvement, so some excellent surgery corrected it without any permanent damage. The keeper was back at work after three months, and ultimately, after a couple of years on the staff, went into veterinary medicine as a career.

The incident had three quite disparate results. The least important—but the most unexpected to me—was the reaction of the press. Knowing the papers' affection for zoo copy, I assumed this was front-page stuff. Here was REAL NEWS! Not so. Without a word being said by anyone involved, the papers buried the whole incident in a short paragraph back in their second sections. Apparently the editors did not wish to impair their readers' image of the zoo as a cheerful place, full of soft, friendly animals where all was love and affection.

The result that was logical and appropriate was a massive reexamination of all the zoo's handling routines. Some of them were altered and all of them were then locked into the most careful and conservative procedures. At the same time, all the display areas and cages were checked and occasionally modified for potential danger to the visiting public. If such a price can ever be justified, a case can be made that the incident may have prevented an even greater disaster later on. As it is, so far as I know, there was never another accident to either staff or the public at the Wichita Zoo.

But the most dramatic result was the impact on Father and Mr. MacDonald. As might have been expected, they reacted in precisely opposite directions. MacDonald was shocked and outraged. This was just what might have been expected from all this foolishness. This playing around with the zoo had ended in tragedy . . . the worst possible outcome from what was a harebrained idea in the first place. Father was equally shaken and was convinced that the incident had only one meaning: he'd fiddled around with bits and pieces long enough. It was time that the whole idea was faced up to in an adult, businesslike manner. It was time that the little zoo was converted from a casual bunch of pets under the trees to a professional, integrated zoological garden, staffed with knowledgeable experts and operated by professional standards. MacDonald said wipe it out, Father said treble it. Complete breakdown of communication at last.

The conflict had been building through the past months until it had finally settled down to a firm feud. As the front man, the activist, the giver of talks and initiator of programs, Father had built up a sympathetic reputation among the community. The businessmen liked what he was doing, the school people thought he "understood their problems," and the ladies' clubs loved to hear him tell about kids and furry animals. On the other hand, MacDonald was still the boss, still had the Park Board with him to a man—and to my detached and objective view, was right about sixty percent of the time!

The old argument over how to use the park land had roared louder than ever. For every stretch of greensward in the city, Father had detailed drawings of roque courts, horseshoe pits, concrete chess tables with benches, shuffleboards, picnic tables, and the ubiquitous tennis courts. Poor Mr. MacDonald was struggling to keep oases of trees and walks and fountains and flower gardens, fuming in his red-faced way in favor of beauty, while Father clothed himself in the righteousness of use.

As a dispassionate observor from the supper table, I marveled at their unending dedication to the public. While it was true the parks were being used as never before, it seemed to me that they produced a disheartening number of atrocity stories come evening. Shortly after Labor Day we got the report of the three carloads of high school kids who'd driven off across the Municipal Golf Course the night before to race around the numbered flags. When they finally lost interest, they had destroyed three grass greens costing over six thousand dollars each. Early in October, Charlie Peterson made his 2 A.M. check of the airport grounds and discovered someone had removed eight hundred chrysanthemum plants set out the day before in front of the terminal building.

The first week of November, Father found every park bench from all the parks south of Douglas and east of Hydraulic—some sixty of them—thrown over a six-foot chain-link fence into the empty swimming pool at College Hill

Park. And by Christmas, Mr. MacDonald had watched his forty-first blue spruce cut off at the base to decorate, we assumed, the forty-first household for the holidays. Between racing from park to park to protect the evergreens and clearing out the kids necking in the parking lots, poor Peterson was on the verge of tears every night. From where I sat, I'd have given the whole thing up in disgust, but neither Father nor MacDonald flagged a bit in their determination to provide beauty and delight to our fellow citizens.

And Father was headed for the final assault toward his dream of the zoo. Like any good public servant, Father was sure he knew what the citizens really wanted, but as was so often the case, they simply did not realize it. It was his obligation to let them see their opportunity so they could embrace it as their own, and award themselves the satisfaction of an immediate job well done and a future of service to their own children and their community. He was going to let them build a zoo for the town, and he was going to do it through the service clubs of the city.

There are few more pitiful specimens than a program chairman of a service club. Rotary meets every week at Tuesday noon, so of course Kiwanis must make every Thursday. This leaves Monday noons for Civitan, Wednesday noons for the Lions, and Friday for the Optimist Club. The Elks, Shriners, VFW, American Legion, and Masons have to have one community-service program a month, and the ladies of the Eastern Star, P.E.O., D.A.R., and Twentieth Century Club are equally devoted to civic betterment and/or inspirational guidance. The program chairman's problem is that he is not given a thin dime to pay anyone with, but he's got to come up with forty-odd luncheon speakers drawn from the same middle-sized community every year.

This is no mean feat. Once you've had the secretary of the Red Cross Chapter, the local director of the National Foundation, and the chairman of the Community Chest, things begin to toughen up. Though the ministerial community is free, you can't work it too hard without antagonizing too many faiths in the club. You don't dare get into politics. The group tends one way, but there's an enormous range within that tend. And you can only use the visiting scholarship students just so often. So, for the same reason it's so big in the local papers, the zoo-and-park man is a sure thing at least once each season at every club.

Father exploited this opportunity as a reflex action. As a long-time recreational sort (he'd worked with the YMCA, the Boy Scouts, in settlement houses, and in school systems before he got into the park business), one of his basic tenets was that the people didn't know what was good for them. As a teen-ager, I used to writhe in embarrassment watching him organize a sport. Let's start a bowling league! At night, after work, he'd start calling the action elite of Coleman Lamp and Stove Company, Red Star Milling Co., Cudahy Packing Plant, the Baptist Alliance, and what-have-you. In every case the presentation was the same. He knew how busy George was, and Heaven knew if there was anyone who didn't need something else to do at night it was George and nobody knew it better than Bernie did. HOWEVER, there was a bunch of people at Coleman . . . Red Star . . . Cudahy's . . . that were terribly lonely, who night after night sat at home listening to the radio . . . knew no one . . . never spoke a friendly word. If only George would help him get a program started . . . just get it rolling for one season, what an enormous impact it would have. Would you give me some names and a little help just this once, George? George invariably would.

The next week, through my homework, I'd hear the conversations continue. Bill, George is trying to set up a bowling league there at C . . . R . . . C . . . and the poor guy is working so hard at it, and it means so much to him, I wonder if you'd give him a little help just this once? I know you're not particularly interested in bowling yourself, but for George's sake, could you give him just one night a week? Forty calls later, he'd have half the plant doing it to keep somebody else from being disappointed.

As a kid, this glib hypocrisy used to put me in agony—and I could never understand why it was that five years later, every last one of the team was still bowling every week (volleyball . . . baseball . . . dancing . . . whatever he'd conned them into) and it was the greatest thing in their lives! Now he was going to let them build a zoo, and it was time to get down to the nitty-gritty of hard money.

Father sketched out his zoo in detail on long sheets of shelf paper. The cloudy Children's Farm hardened into clear pictures of rabbits living in the Old Lady's Shoe House. Pink pigs were given three bright houses of wood, straw, and bricks. Billy Goat Gruff got an arched bridge to live under. Father couldn't make up his mind whether the cow would have the milkmaid motif or the dish-and-spoon theme, but there would be one cow. There would be donkey rides. Possibly a goat cart. Obviously sheep and Bo-Peep. It got more and more elaborate—and then was presented to the American Legion as their fund raising purpose for the coming year. Kiwanis got the seal and sea lion pool. The Civitans the monkey island. The Shriners the zebra-llama-camel house. And so through the program.

Father never gave the faintest hint of any of this to Mr. MacDonald who would have been outraged at the use of the land, much less the expansionist theme throughout, and who was still shaken by the bear incident . . . But as Father would take his "What's Going On In Your Parks" lecture to each meeting, it would start out with the water regattas, work through the sports programs, touch on the outdoor plays, concerts, and operettas for culture, and end up with the zoo. To hear Father tell it, the zoo had reduced juvenile delinquency by half, cut the divorce rate, increased church attendance, and redistributed the tax base by increasing out-of-city revenues. And each speech ended up with, "And there's a crying need for a new——, which can't be had without your group giving it to the children of Wichita." The details were then sketched in as an afterthought.

By midwinter of my freshman year, Father had sown these seeds throughout the town. He had all the proper committees brooding on the possibilities, and creeping up to the decision point. At this juncture, we got the theme for the first time at home.

"Mae, I need something dramatic. Something that'll jar 'em from wouldn't-it-be-nice-to to let's-do-it! If only there was something that could be done without money! The investment of just a little right now would bring in so much later. We need something big. What should a zoo have that really symbolizes a zoo? What can we get that when people talk about it, it paints a whole picture all by itself?"

Long silence while Mother cringed and I wondered where he was headed.

"An elephant would do it, but it's out of the question. Even if we could get our hands on one, there's no place to put it. No, not an elephant. But a tiger? By gosh, a big, fat, striped tiger, with fangs and a lashing tail? I think that's it! The Lion House'd hold him. Yessir, that's it! I gotta have a tiger. An enormous tiger! Where can I get a tiger . . . and get it past MacDonald? Where can I. . . ."

We watched him, uneasy but intrigued.

Nowdays, here in the late Sixties, a tiger sells for something over two thousand dollars, and while dollars went a good deal farther in the Thirties, in the case of tigers there wasn't as much difference as might be imagined. In those days any tigers that had to be imported came by sea, and the cost of the passage, plus the increased mortality, almost made our present, airborne imports "cheap." The point for Father was that Trefflich's was selling tigers for slightly more than the Chief of Police was making in his annual salary, and the possibility of our trading anything we had for a new tiger or even an old one was flat out nil.

Into this milieu came a tiny AP release that turned up in the Sunday *Beacon.* Father read it and was instantly convinced that we are all part of a Divine Plan. There it was in black and white: a little third-string circus had caught fire while playing a small town near Atlanta. The owners had declared bankruptcy and pulled out, leaving the local sheriff with a mound of blackened canvas and numerous wild, hungry animals. Father rose straight into the air like a flushed pheasant.

"They've got to have one! They've just got to!"

He dashed to the phone and put in a long-distance call to the place. The operator had considerable difficulty finding the town, and even more finding the sheriff, but ultimately Father was tied to a deep Southern accent and asking, "Do you have a tiger there?"

The sheriff admitted he did.

"How much do you want for him?"

The sheriff told him.

"I'll take it, I'll take it! Don't do a thing. I'll wire confirmation at once."

Father hung up and turned around.

"Mae! I've bought a tiger!"

"That's nice. But what will Mr. MacDonald say?"

"It doesn't make any difference what he says. I didn't say I've bought *him* a tiger. I bought it for myself!"

"*You're* going to pay for it? How much does it cost?"

Father casually gave her the figure, which slightly exceeded two years' payments on our house. With Mother teetering on the edge of hysteria, he made soothing remarks about getting bargain tigers at fire sales. He then sent our Christmas Savings Club money to Georgia as down payment.

Two weeks later we were down at the Railway Express Company again, but what a difference from the lovebirds and the coatimondi! This time there were photographers from both papers, the zoo truck all washed and shined, and the Express Company was as excited as we were. All their brass was on hand and when the 5:00 Santa Fe from Tulsa arrived, we found the men in the baggage car picturing themselves as big-game importers straight out of Frank Buck.

The tiger was there for all to see, shipped in an iron-barred cage on little wheels which apparently had been used to move the beast from its circus wagon into the center ring wild animal act and back again. He was pacing back and forth, teeth bared and tail lashing just like Father had pictured—though with slightly more ribs showing than was quite appropriate. Several of the baggage men seized the pulling tongue on the wagon and, giving it a wide berth on the back and sides, got it pulled onto a platform freight wagon and then the two together rolled to the zoo truck. Many pictures and much excitement. Down Douglas Avenue, the main drag, in slow and triumphant procession. On to the zoo where half the cats had been moved around to give the tiger the balancing cage at the other end from Simba. When the shipping cage was properly positioned, Saylor pried the end up and the tiger leaped into the open cage with a savage snarl which gave Father all the fury he could hope for. The two leopards and all three lions took an instant hatred of the intruder and the roaring and spitting and clawing about was bedlam. Father was delighted.

The next morning Father rushed to the office to see MacDonald before the papers appeared and blithely told him that he had become convinced the zoo had to have a tiger to form a base for the major upgrading of the collection. He'd been hearing a great deal of enthusiastic comments from the service clubs around town who seemed eager to expand the zoo at their own expense. Recognizing that a small investment in an animal like a tiger at this point would produce a great quantity of contributions later, he, Bernie, had decided to make a gift of a tiger to the City of Wichita. Recognizing, however, that some people in the community might think it inappropriate for a civil servant to be personally involved in property transactions with the city, he had told the papers that this was an anonymous donation, and he was eager that he be given no credit for the gift.

MacDonald was apoplectic. He knew he was being taken, but try as he would, he couldn't see just how. There certainly was no law against accepting donations—he'd been doing that ever since the pelican—and as long as . . . With the greatest reluctance he prepared the formal press release and drafted a report to the Park Board.

The newspapers rose to the occasion with a flourish. The *Beacon*—on its own initiative—inaugurated a Name-the-Tiger contest, open to any Wichitan aged ten or younger. The leading merchants contributed small prizes. Daily pictures of the tiger kept the contest going and swelled the zoo crowds. By the close of the month, the contest had been concluded, the tiger named, and if there was anyone in the city that did not know the zoo was alive and thriving, he was illiterate and cut off from all contact with human life.

At this point Father was called upon to make the second payment on the tiger. The truth was, of course, that he had no money to cover it, and he proceeded to explain this to Mr. MacDonald with immoderate embarrassment. "I'm just afraid I'm going to have to send the tiger back to Georgia. I simply can't meet the payments."

NOW Mr. MacDonald knew how he was being taken.

"You know sputter-wheeze well you can't pull that animal out of there after all this fuss. If you get rid of it, there'll be a hell of a yell for another just like it. Those things cost thousands of dollars!"

"Well, actually, not this one. If you're going to have to buy one eventually, anyway, it really would be cheaper to hang on to the one we have, Mr. MacDonald. Through an unusually fortuitous set of circumstances, I was able to pick ours up for only. . . ."

There was considerable discussion in this vein which ended with MacDonald agreeing to go to the Park Board for the money, but with a heartfelt promise that he would not forget this incident (the word "blackmail" kept recurring) if my father worked for him for a hundred years, which at the moment did not seem likely. The Park Board accepted the situation handsomely. The City kept the tiger, which returned the hospitality by getting sleek and fat, pacing back and forth, and snarling to the delight of the largest crowds the zoo had ever seen!

# 13

# *Epilogue*

And that's all there is to the story! Father's zoo career was sort of like life. It's rarely as bad as it might be, but then it seldom comes off with the flourish it should, either.

The tiger arrived in the summer of 1939. By September of that year, the war had broken out in Europe, and almost immediately Wichita's airplane factories shifted to a wartime footing nearly two years before the rest of the country. First with French and British purchases, then with Lend-Lease, and finally with our own rearmament, Boeing, Beechcraft, and Cessna exploded into 80,000 employees.

The city fathers—and the service clubs—immediately became preoccupied with housing another 100,000 new citizens. The Park Department was overwhelmed with building new airports and new parks as the town shot out in all directions across the prairie, and Father's ideas for a great new zoo evaporated out of everybody's mind—including his own.

We Goodrums were swept up in the war effort like everyone else. Father went to work with the USO, setting up hospital rehabilitation centers throughout the Middle West. My freshman class and I were moved off to Ft. Leavenworth and into the Army. The "Incubator House" was sold and so were the incubator, brooders, and pens. None of our family ever lived in Wichita again.

The zoo's momentum slackened to a crawl. Father's animals entertained a decade of war babies and then one after another died of old age and was not replaced. The Bird House became more and more of a menace and was finally pulled down and cannas planted in the foundations. By the Fifties, the zoo was back to the point where Father had found it.

For the next ten years hardly anything happened at all. The Lion House was maintained, the Bear Pits had an occasional small black bear, and the alligators went on as near to death as ever but not quite. Then in the early Sixties, a group of citizens began to ask, "Whatever happened to the zoo?" Various clusters of interest developed. A service club tried to generate attention. A group of business men attempted to get something going. The Park Department made appeals. Each effort came to nothing. Zoos are far more expensive than they were in Father's time!

Came 1965, and suddenly each section of interest seized on to the edge of the next one and they all began to move together. The *Wichita Beacon* got behind a city-county-citizen program of "Our New Zoo Is Overdue." A zoo architect was hired, new sites were explored, and matching funds from the federal Open Spaces Program were sought. The old traditional zoo stories broke out again, this time illustrated with four-color renderings. The prices were breathtaking, but the text read like Father's old shelf-paper dream plans:

$325,000 for large mammal house and paddock
$324,500 for primate house
$185,400 for small mammal, tropical birds and rain forest exhibits
$179,000 for children's zoo
$75,000 for sea lion pool
$245,750 for reptile and aquatic building
$300,000 for bear and cat cages
$90,000 for waterfowl lagoon

Apparently the time was finally ripe, for 1966 closed with the citizens voting a $3,600,000 bond issue to create a new park and zoo—one that would be "the showplace of Mid-continent America." After almost 30 years, Father's fantasies were becoming a reality at last.

Mr. MacDonald has passed away, and Father is retired now, living in another part of the country. I was recently giving him the latest word from Wichita-in-laws about the progress of the new zoo. I noted with awe that all those hundreds of thousands of dollars would merely buy the plant! Funds for the animals must come from yet another source. Father listened to the report with a satisfied smile, and then his eyes flashed.

"Chuck," he said, "with a little imagination there's no reason they can't stock that place in no time. Now if they could just get someone to give them a pelican . . ." I nodded. I had passed this way before.

The End